The Brandon Guide for

Revise with **CLUESS** (pronounce as   ).

Coherence: Establish clear links between ideas. Use words such as *However, Otherwise, Therefore, Similarly, Hence, On the other hand, Then, Consequently, Also,* Thus. pp. 38–41, 197–199, 209

Language: Use words that fit your purpose and audience. Avoid slang, clichés, and vague words and phrases. pp. 184–191, 206

Unity: Stay on your topic. Use strong topic sentences and theses. pp. 192–200

Emphasis: Call attention to important ideas. Repeat key words and phrases, often placing them near the beginning or end of a sentence, paragraph, or essay. pp. 78–84, 192–199

Support: Back up your controlling idea with evidence and logic. pp. 192–198, 206–219

Sentences: Write correct, effective sentences with structural variety. pp. 27–57, 197

Edit with **CGPS** (pronounce as "see GPS" for easy memorization).

Capitalization: pp. 172–174

Grammar: pp. 1–151

Punctuation: pp. 38, 40, 152–172

Spelling: pp. 178–189

Brandon Writing Process Worksheet

Title _____

Name _____ Due Date _____

Assignment
(Use separate
paper if
needed.)

In the space below, write whatever you need to know about your assignment, including information about the topic, audience, pattern of writing, length, whether to include a rough draft or revised drafts, and whether your paper must be typed.

Stage One

Explore Freewrite, list, cluster, or take notes as directed by your instructor.

Stage Two

Organize Write a topic sentence or thesis; label the subject and focus parts.

Write an outline or an outline alternative. For reading-based writing, include references and short quotations with page numbers as support in the outline.

Stage Three
(Check off
the ten parts
of CLUESS
and CGPS as
you complete
revising and
editing.)

Write On separate paper, write and then revise your paragraph or essay as many times as necessary for **c**oherence □, **l**anguage (usage, tone, and diction) □, **u**nity □, **e**mphasis □, **s**upport □, and **s**entences □ (**CLUESS**). **Edit** problems in fundamentals, such as **c**apitalization □, **g**rammar □, **p**unctuation □, and **s**pelling □ (**CGPS**). **Read** your work aloud to hear and correct any structural errors or awkward-sounding sentences.

At a Glance

Writing Sentences and Beyond

SIXTH EDITION

Lee Brandon
Mt. San Antonio College

Kelly Brandon
Santa Ana College

Australia • Brazil • Japan • Korea • Mexico • Singapore • Spain • United Kingdom • United States

CENGAGE
Learning®

To Sharon

At a Glance: Writing Sentences and Beyond, Sixth Edition

Lee Brandon, Kelly Brandon

Product Director: Annie Todd

Managing Developer: Megan Garvey

Development Editor: Margaret Manos

Content Coordinator: Elizabeth Rice

Product Assistant: Luria Rittenberg

Marketing Brand Manager: Lydia LeStar

Senior Content Project Manager: Aimee Chevrette Bear

Art Director: Faith Brosnan

Manufacturing Planner: Betsy Donaghey

Rights Acquisition Specialist: Ann Hoffman

Production Service: Books By Design, Inc.

Cover Designer: Walter Kopec, Boston

Cover Image: Eddie Hironaka/ Photographer's Choice/Getty Images

Compositor: S4Carlisle Publishing Services

Library of Congress Control Number: 2013941276

ISBN-13: 978-1-285-44465-9
ISBN-10: 1-285-44465-5

Cengage Learning
200 First Stamford Place, 4th Floor
Stamford, CT 06902
USA

Cengage Learning is a leading provider of customized learning solutions with office locations around the globe, including Singapore, the United Kingdom, Australia, Mexico, Brazil, and Japan. Locate your local office at **international.cengage.com/region.**

Cengage Learning products are represented in Canada by Nelson Education, Ltd.

For your course and learning solutions, visit **www.cengage.com.**

Purchase any of our products at your local college store or at our preferred online store **www.cengagebrain.com.**

Instructors: Please visit **login.cengage.com** and log in to access instructor-specific resources.

Printed in the United States of America
1 2 3 4 5 6 7 17 16 15 14 13

Contents

Preface

In this, the sixth edition of *At a Glance: Writing Sentences and Beyond*, the surf writer, gallantly perched on a pencil, celebrates the "flow of writing." Like waves at a beach, writing is cyclical, moving forward and backward and forward again. As the students' guide and muse, the surf writer will always be searching for the "perfect wave," meaning the best possible expression—one that is correct and effective. The controlled recursive movements of prewriting, organization, writing, revision, and editing are the essence of that relentless search.

At a Glance: Writing Sentences and Beyond is the first-level book in the *At a Glance* series. Along with *At a Glance: Writing Paragraphs and Beyond with Integrated Readings*, *At a Glance: Writing Essays and Beyond with Integrated Readings*, and *At a Glance: Reader*, it features sentence writing, but includes basic instruction in writing paragraphs, short essays, and summaries. It is thoroughly up to date with broad coverage and innovative instruction, yet it is highly affordable. Each of the four books provides basic writing instruction, exercises, and writing assignments at the designated level, as well as support material for instructors. *At a Glance: Writing Sentences and Beyond* and *At a Glance: Writing Paragraphs and Beyond* include smooth transitions to the next level of writing. *At a Glance: Writing Paragraphs and Beyond,*and *At a Glance: Writing Essays and Beyond* each concludes with a handbook that students can refer to for help with sentence-level issues or for problems with mechanics. *At a Glance: Reader* presents brief writing instruction and thirty sources for critical analysis, modeling, and reading-based writing. Each book in the *At a Glance* series can be used alone, with one of the other *At a Glance* books, or with another textbook. Two or more *At a Glance* books can be shrink-wrapped and delivered at a discount, and *At a Glance: Reader* costs only half price when ordered shrink-wrapped with another *At a Glance* book.

∿ New and Enhanced Material in This Edition

New! The Brandon Guide for Revising and Editing

Look just inside the front cover at the first three pages:

- On the inside front cover, you will find the **Self-Evaluation Chart for the Brandon guide** for students to record problems and progress in revising and editing (discussed in the Student Overview, page xiii, and in Chapter 12, page 197).

- On the next page, page A-1, you will find a list of **the Brandon Guide principles** along with acronyms for easily recalling and completing revising and editing: **CLUESS** (pronounced "clues" and representing *C*oherence, *L*anguage, *U*nity, *E*mphasis, *S*upport, and *S*entences for revision) and **CGPS** (pronounced "see GPS" and representing *C*apitalization, *G*rammar, *P*unctuation, and *S*pelling for editing). The Brandon Guide is offered to help students organize and write their paragraphs and essays, to provide a framework of standards for peer editing and cooperative assignments, and to state features of good writing that can be used (with appropriate modifications) in instructor-student conferences and classroom instruction, and even for departmental and campus-wide objectives.

- On page A-2 is the **Brandon Writing Process Worksheet**. It can be enlarged and printed for students to use in following the three stages of writing—Explore, Organize, Write. The completed worksheet can be attached to the student writing, providing a documented view of how the student proceeded in completing an assignment. Filled in by the student before the actual writing, it can reveal to the instructor how well the student understands the assignment. The instructor can also customize the large page-size Word copy on the Instructor Companion Site to fit his or her pedagogy or to work on particular assignments. Students will find a printable, large page-size worksheet online at ***www.cengagebrain.com***.

New! Chapter 13: "Writing a Summary"

- A discussion of the definition of a summary, ten rules in writing a good summary, and a demonstration with practice for the student.
- A lesson to be taught on the difference between writing an analysis and a summary and the difference between original and plagiarized writing.

New! How to Write a Paragraph or an Essay of Classification

- This textbook includes all ten patterns of organization. See Chapter 14.

New! Seventeen New Exercises in Sentence Writing Within Chapters 1–11

New! Additional Topics in Chapters 12 and 14 for Writing Paragraphs and Essays

Instructional Approach for Writing Sentences

In Chapters 1–11 of *At a Glance: Writing Sentences and Beyond*, contextual exercises explore contemporary, informative, culturally diverse, and even deliberately humorous topics selected to engage students' interests. Principles, rules, and guidelines are explained concisely and are supported directly with appropriate examples. Each unit of sentence writing concludes with a review consisting of additional practice and, when appropriate, directs students to write original sentences. The Instructor's Guide provides a diagnostic test, a final examination, and unit quizzes that can be given as tests or used as additional exercises.

Instructional Approach for Writing Paragraphs and Short Essays

Using examples and concise instruction along with more than a hundred topics, Chapters 12, 13, and 14 provide the framework for working on sentences in the contexts of paragraph, summary, and essay assignments. The Brandon Writing Process Worksheet lists and explains the stages of writing. Patterns of writing, combined patterns of writing, and summary writing help guide organization necessary for particular assignments. The Brandon Guide for Revising and Editing provides guidance for student writers and establishes a rubric for their peer-editing and cooperative work projects.

⌒ Free Material for Instructors

Instructor Companion Site

- This site at ***www.cengagebrain.com*** also presents helpful re-sources in addition to an Answer Key to the book, the Instruc-tor's Guide, PowerPoint slides, and a transition guide linking editions.

Instructor's Guide

- Available online on the Instructor Companion Site at Cengage Learning, Higher Education or at ***www.cengagebrain.com***.
- Provides helpful suggestions for teaching *At a Glance* books in the classroom. It includes sample syllabi, suggestions for working with basic writing students and ESL students, grading tips, sets of charts and guides, answer keys, eighty sets of quiz-zes and answers on sentence writing, longer readings and other units of instruction, handbook material, and more.

⌒ Free Material for Students

- **Student Companion Site for *At a Glance* at *www.cengagebrain .com*.** The student site provides helpful resources such as an MLA guide and an APA guide to documented papers, a printable Writing Process Worksheet, a printable Self-Evaluation Chart for the Brandon Guide, tips on writing résumés and letters of application, skills in taking tests, and more.

⌒ Acknowledgments

We are profoundly indebted to the many instructors who have reviewed *At a Glance: Writing Sentences and Beyond* for these six editions and helped it grow and remain fresh and innovative. Here are a few of those thoughtful and imaginative reviewers: Kate Brubeck (and her students), Mills College; Allison Alison, South-eastern Community College; Laura Peet, Bakersfield College; Marsha Elyn Wright, Garden City Community College; Cindi Clarke, Belmont Technical College; Tim Kelley, Northwest-Shoals Community College; Darin Cozzens, Surry Community

College; James Crooks, Shasta College; Deborah Burson-Smith, Southern University at New Orleans; Karen A. Cahill, Southeastern Community College; Iris Gribble-Neal, Eastern Washington University; Ardyce Ketterling, Bismark State College; Tamara Kuzmankov, Tacoma Community College; David Lang, Golden Gate University; Lynette Lochasusen, Colorado Mountain College; Phyllis MacCameron, Erie Community College; Kathy Masters, Arkansas State University; Sharon Owens, University of Texas at El Paso; Dianne Perkins, Community College of Philadelphia; John Richardson, Augusta Technical College; Judith Sinclair, Catholic University; Alice Steilder, Santa Barbara City College; Marilyn Strauss, Pace University; Steve Stremmel, American River College; Pamela A. Tackaburg, Fullerton College; David White, Walters State Community College; Marilyn Black, Middlesex Community College; Julie M. Kissel, Washtenaw Community College; Pat Leverentz, Pima Community College; Vern Lindquist, Sullivan County Community College; Laurel E. Spillum, Portland Community College; and Elin Tomov, Georgia Perimeter College.

We also deeply appreciate the expert, dedicated work of Principal Editor Margaret Manos; Production Manager Nancy Benjamin with Books By Design; Editorial Specialist Ann Marie McNeely; Permissions Editor Christina Taylor; and our colleagues at Cengage Learning: Director of Developmental Studies Annie Todd, Editorial Assistant Luria Rittenburg, Assistant Editor Elizabeth Rice, and Senior Content Project Manager Aimee Chevrette Bear.

We are especially grateful to family members for their cheerful, inspiring support: Sharon, Kelly, Erin, Michael, Kathy, Jessica, Deborah, Shane, Lauren, Jarrett, and Matthew.

Lee Brandon
Kelly Brandon

Student Overview

The first in a series of *At a Glance* books, this concise, contemporary, affordable volume is designed to help you write correct and effective sentences both separately and in context. We hope you will find this book enjoyable and instructive.

- In Chapters 1 through 6, you'll work with understanding sentence parts, identifying kinds of sentences, putting short sentences together to show relationships, fixing groups of words that look like sentences but really are not, and balancing the parts of a sentence.
- In Chapters 7 through 11, you'll study how to make the most effective use of verbs, pronouns, adjectives and adverbs, punctuation and capitalization, and spelling.
- In Chapter 12, you'll look at the writing process as a series of steps that can carry you from stage to stage until you have produced a polished paragraph or essay.
- In Chapter 13, you'll learn to write summaries, highlighting the main ideas and avoiding plagiarism.
- In Chapter 14, you'll find instructions and more than a hundred topics for writing with specific and combined patterns of paragraphs and essays.

Here are some strategies to help you make the best use of this book and to jump-start the improvement in your writing skills.

1. **Evaluate your writing skills.** After paragraphs or short essays are marked and returned to you, and after you have worked with exercises and quizzes, use the **Self-Evaluation Chart for the Brandon Guide** inside the front cover of this book to list areas you need to work on. On the page facing the Self-Evaluation Chart, page A-1, you will see a list of principles for revising and editing. A larger form can be downloaded from the online Student Companion Site at ***www.cengagebrain.com***. You can add to your lists throughout the entire quarter or semester. Drawing on your instructor's

comments, make notes on matters of revising, as indicated by the easily remembered acronym CLUESS (pronounced "clues"): Coherence, Language, Unity, Emphasis, Support, and Sentences (as in style). Using what you are learning in this book about writing sentences, you can make notes with page number references on matters of editing included in the acronym CGPS (pronounced "see GPS"): Capitalization, Grammar, Punctuation, and Spelling. As you master a problem, you can mark it off or erase it to show your progress.

Here is an example of a partially completed Self-Evaluation Chart.

Self-Evaluation Chart for the Brandon Guide					
Revise with CLUESS (pronounced as "clues")					
Coherence	Language	Unity	Emphasis	Support	Sentences
Use transitions, pp. 40–41	No trite words, p. 195	Topic sentence, p. 193	Repeat key word, p. 197	Use examples, p. 207	Vary sentence beginnings, p. 52
Edit with CGPS (pronounced as "see GPS")					
Capitalization: I'm studying biology, English, and math. p. 172					
Grammar: Pronoun case: between you and me. p. 119					
Punctuation: After she left, I cried. p. 154					
Spelling: It's or its? There or their? Receive or receive? p. 178					

2. **Use the Brandon Writing Process Worksheet for writing paragraphs and essays** that appears on page A-2. An enlarged copy can be downloaded from the Student Companion Site. Using the worksheet, you can easily record details about each of your assignments, such as the due date, topic, length, and form, and then work systematically on the stages of the writing process: **Explore** (your topic), **Organize** (as an outlined plan), and **Write** (rough draft, revisions, and edits).

3. **Be positive. Don't compare yourself with others.** Compare yourself with yourself and, as you make progress, consider what you are—a student on the path toward effective writing, a student on the road to success.

1

Parts of Speech

Why does this book begin with parts of speech? The answer is twofold:

- First, the parts of speech are the most basic word units you will work with in this book. Here at the outset you will learn, or review, how parts of speech function in communicating ideas, and what you can and cannot do effectively with each one in your writing. Knowing parts of speech is one of your gateways to experimenting with confidence in writing. Your understanding of them will be reinforced in each of the following chapters.
- Second, knowing the names of the parts of speech will allow you to discuss the language you use and will help you understand your instructors' comments on writing, specifically on *your* writing. This principle can be applied to all areas of learning. Knowing terminology enables you to communicate with others. In discussing computers, for example, without knowing basic terminology—*mouse, booting, desktop, Internet Explorer, username, gigabyte*—you would be tongue-tied when you were trying to learn or needed technical help. The same goes for you as a student of writing. By the time you have finished this book, you will know parts of speech well.

To classify a word as a part of speech, we observe two simple principles:

1. The word must be in the context of communication, usually in a sentence. The first principle is important because some words can be any of several parts of speech. The word *round*, for example, can function as five:

    - I watched the potter *round* the block of clay. (verb)
    - I saw her go *round* the corner. (preposition)
    - She has a *round* head. (adjective)

- The astronauts watched the world go *round*. (adverb)
- The champ knocked him out in one *round*. (noun)

2. We must be able to distinguish the word from other parts of speech that have their own characteristics: nouns, pronouns, verbs, adjectives, adverbs, prepositions, conjunctions, or interjections.

Nouns

Nouns are naming words. Nouns may name persons, animals, plants, places, things, substances, qualities, or ideas—for example, *Bart, armadillo, zombie, tree, rock, cloud, love, ghost, music,* and *virtue.*

Nouns are often pointed out by noun indicators. These noun indicators—*the, a, an*—signal that a noun is ahead, although there may be words between the indicator and the noun itself.

the slime	*a* werewolf	*an* aardvark
the green slime	*a* hungry werewolf	*an* angry aardvark

Pronouns

A **pronoun** is a word that is used in place of a noun.

- Some pronouns may represent specific persons or things:

I	she	they	you
me	her	them	yourself
myself	herself	themselves	yourselves
it	he	we	who
itself	him	us	whom
that	himself	ourselves	

- Indefinite pronouns refer to nouns (persons, places, things) in a general way:

each	everyone	nobody	somebody

- Other pronouns point out particular things:

SINGULAR *this, that* PLURAL *these, those*
This is my treasure. *These* are my jewels.
That is your stuff. *Those* are your trinkets.

- Still other pronouns introduce questions.

  Which is the best CD player?

  What are the main ingredients of a Twinkie?

〜 Verbs

Verbs show action or express being in relation to the subject of a sentence. They customarily occur in set positions in sentences.

- **Action verbs** are usually easy to identify.

  The aardvark *ate* the crisp, tasty ants. (action verb)

  The aardvark *washed* them down with a snoutful of water. (action verb)

- The ***being*** **verbs** are few in number and are also easy to identify. The most common *being* verbs are *is*, *was*, *were*, *are*, and *am*.

  Harry Potter lives in a fictional universe. (*being* verb)

  I *am* his enthusiastic fan. (*being* verb)

- The form of a verb expresses its tense, that is, the time of the action or being. The time may be in the present or past.

  Bruce Springsteen *sings* "Born to Run." (present)

  Bruce Springsteen *sang* "Born to Run." (past)

- One or more **helping verbs** may be used with the main verb to form other tenses. The combination is called a **verb phrase**.

  He *has sung* the song many times for huge crowds in stadiums. (Helping verb and main verb indicate a time in the past.)

  He *will be singing* the song many more times while on tours. (Helping verbs and main verb indicate a time in the future.)

- Some helping verbs can be used alone as main verbs: *has*, *have*, *had*, *is*, *was*, *were*, *are*, and *am*. Certain other helping verbs function only as helpers: *will*, *shall*, *should*, and *could*.

  The most common position for the verb is directly after the subject or after the subject and its modifiers.

  At high noon only two men [subject] *were* on Main Street.

  The man with the faster draw [subject and modifiers] *walked* away alone.

∿ Adjectives

- **Adjectives** modify nouns and pronouns. Most adjectives answer the questions *What kind? Which one?* and *How many?* Adjectives answering the *What kind?* question are descriptive. They tell the quality, kind, or condition of the nouns or pronouns they modify.

red convertible	*dirty* fork
noisy muffler	*wild* roses
The rain is *gentle.*	Bob was *tired.*

- Adjectives answering the *Which one?* question narrow or restrict the meaning of a noun. Some of these are pronouns that become adjectives by function.

my money	*our* ideas	the *other* house
this reason	*these* apples	

- Adjectives answering the *How many?* question are, of course, numbering words.

some people	*each* pet	*few* goals
three dollars	*one* glove	

- The words *a, an,* and *the* are adjectives called **articles.** As "noun indicators," they point out persons, places, and things.

∿ Adverbs

Adverbs modify (describe or explain) verbs, adjectives, and other adverbs. Adverbs answer the questions *How? Where? When?* and *To what degree?*

MODIFYING VERBS	They <u>did</u> their work <u>quickly</u>.
	$\quad$v$\qquad\qquad\qquad\;$adv
	He <u>replied</u> <u>angrily</u>.
	$\;$v$\qquad$adv
MODIFYING ADJECTIVES	They were <u>somewhat</u> <u>happy</u>.
	$\qquad\qquad$adv$\qquad$adj
MODIFYING ADVERBS	She answered <u>very</u> <u>slowly</u>.
	$\qquad\qquad$adv$\quad$adv

- Adverbs that answer the *How?* question are concerned with manner or way.

   Irena ate the burgers *hungrily.*   Moe snored *noisily.*

- Adverbs that answer the *Where?* question show location.

   They drove *downtown.*   Loretta climbed *upstairs.*
   Joseph stayed *behind.*

- Adverbs that answer the *When?* question indicate time.

   The ship sailed *yesterday.*   I expect an answer *soon.*

- Adverbs that answer the *To what degree?* question express extent.

   Barbara is *entirely* correct.   Pete was *somewhat* annoyed.

Most words ending in *-ly* are adverbs.

   Ramon completed the task <u>skillfully</u>.
   adv

   Silvia answered him <u>courteously</u>.
   adv

However, there are a few exceptions.

   The house provided a <u>lovely</u> view of the valley.
   adj

   Your intimidation mask is <u>ugly</u>.
   adj

∿ Prepositions

A **preposition** is a word or group of words that function as a connective. The preposition connects its object(s) to some other word(s) in the sentence. A preposition and its object(s)—usually a noun or pronoun—with modifiers make up a **prepositional phrase**.

Bart worked <u>against</u> great <u>odds</u>.

prepositional phrase

Everyone <u>in</u> his <u>household</u> cheered his effort.

prepositional phrase

Following are some of the most common prepositions:

about	before	but	into	past
above	behind	by	like	to
across	below	despite	near	toward
after	beneath	down	of	under
against	beside	for	off	until
among	between	from	on	upon
around	beyond	in	over	with

Some prepositions are composed of more than one word and are formed from other parts of speech:

according to	as far as	because of	in spite of
ahead of	as well as	in back of	instead of
along with	aside from	in front of	together with

A prepositional phrase can serve as an adjective or adverb within the sentence structure.

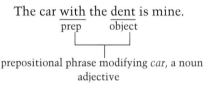

The car with the dent is mine.
     prep   object

prepositional phrase modifying *car*, a noun
adjective

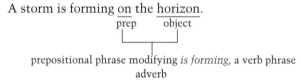

A storm is forming on the horizon.
     prep   object

prepositional phrase modifying *is forming*, a verb phrase
adverb

Caution: Do not confuse adverbs with prepositions.

I went *across* slowly. (without an object—adverb)

I went *across* the field. (with an object—preposition)

We walked *behind* silently. (without an object—adverb)

We walked *behind* the mall. (with an object—preposition)

∿ Conjunctions

A **conjunction** connects and shows a relationship between words, phrases, or clauses. A phrase is two or more words acting as a part of speech. A clause is a group of words with a subject and a verb. An independent clause can stand by itself: *Jolene plays bass guitar.*

A dependent clause cannot stand by itself: *when Jolene plays bass guitar.*

The two kinds of conjunctions are coordinating and subordinating.

Coordinating conjunctions connect words, phrases, and clauses of equal rank: noun with noun, adjective with adjective, verb with verb, phrase with phrase, main clause with main clause, and subordinate clause with subordinate clause. The seven common coordinating conjunctions are *for, and, nor, but, or, yet,* and *so.* (An easy way to remember them is to think of the acronym FANBOYS, which is made up of the first letter of each conjunction.)

TWO NOUNS   Bring a <u>pencil</u> <u>and</u> some <u>paper</u>.
  noun   conj   noun

TWO PHRASES   Did she go <u>to the store</u> <u>or</u> <u>to the game</u>?
  prep phrase conj prep phrase

Paired conjunctions such as *either/or, neither/nor,* or *both/and* are usually classed as coordinating conjunctions.

<u>Neither</u> the coach <u>nor</u> the manager was at fault.
  conj   conj

Subordinating conjunctions connect dependent clauses with main clauses. Here is a list of the most common subordinating conjunctions:

after	because	provided	whenever
although	before	since	where
as	but that	so that	whereas
as if	if	till	wherever
as long as	in order that	until	
as soon as	notwithstanding	when	

If the dependent clause comes *before* the main clause, it is set off by a comma.

<u>Although</u> <u>she</u> <u>was</u> in pain, she stayed in the game.
  conj   subj   v

dependent clause

If the dependent clause comes *after* the main clause, it usually is *not* set off by a comma.

She stayed in the game <u>because</u> <u>she</u> <u>was needed</u>.
  conj   subj   v

dependent clause

Caution: Certain words can function as either conjunctions or prepositions. It is necessary to look ahead to see if the word introduces a clause with a subject and verb—conjunction function—or takes an object—preposition function. Some of the words with two functions are *after, for, since,* and *until.*

> *After* the concert was over, we went home. (clause follows—conjunction)
>
> *After* the concert, we went home. (object follows—preposition)

Interjections

An **interjection** conveys strong emotion or surprise. When an interjection appears alone, it is usually punctuated with an exclamation mark. An interjection can be more than one word, and almost any word or phrase can be an interjection if it is to be charged with feeling.

> Right!   Wow!   Yikes!   Duh!   Cowabunga!   Yoink!   Woo-hoo!

When it appears as part of a sentence, an interjection is usually followed by a comma.

> Oh, I did not consider that problem.

The interjection may be used by the writer to indicate excitement, but the interjection and the exclamation mark should be used only to reflect an emotionally charged message and not to create it.

Chapter Review

Exercise 1   Identifying Parts of Speech

Indicate the part of speech of each italicized word or group of words by placing the appropriate abbreviations in the blanks.

n	noun	pro	pronoun
v	verb	adj	adjective
adv	adverb	conj	conjunction
prep	preposition		

_____ _____ 1. *For* about forty years, the Three Stooges were a popular *comedy* team.

_____ _____ 2. They were *often* accused of making films *in* bad taste, but no one accused them of being good actors.

_____ _____ 3. For decades, they *made seven* or more pictures a year.

_____ _____ 4. Actually six *different* actors *played* the parts.

_____ _____ 5. The *most* famous threesome *was* Moe, Curly, and Larry.

_____ _____ 6. The Stooges specialized *in physical* comedy.

_____ _____ 7. They *took* special *delight* in hitting each other in the head and poking each other's eyes.

_____ _____ 8. Moe was the on-screen *leader* of this *zany* group.

_____ _____ 9. He assumed leadership in each film *because he* was more intelligent than the others, which isn't saying much.

_____ _____ 10. Curly was not bright, but he made up for his *dumbness* by having the *hardest* head in the world, at least in the world of Stooge movies.

_____ _____ 11. Larry *often got caught* between the flailing arms and kicking feet of Moe and Curly.

_____ _____ 12. The movies made *by* the Stooges *usually* came in two reels and were shown along with feature-length films.

_____ _____ 13. The Stooge movies *were given* such *titles* as *Half-Wits, Three Hams on Rye, Slap Happy Sleuths,* and *Matri Phony.*

_____ _____ 14. They made fun of *dignity* and physically abused each other with all kinds *of* lethal instruments, but they never got hurt.

_____ _____ 15. They received *little respect* from the filmmaking community.

_____ _____ 16. Only Moe saved *his* money *and* became wealthy.

_____ _____ 17. Apparently Curly *at* times lived his *movie* role off stage.

_____ _____ 18. After a *brief* marriage, Curly's wife *left* him, saying he punched, poked, pinched, and pushed her and left cigar butts in the sink.

_____ _____ 19. Moe tried to gain *respectability* as a character actor, but the audiences could never accept *him* in serious roles.

_____ _____ 20. A whole new television *audience has made* the Three Stooges the stars they never were in their lifetimes.

Exercise 2   Identifying Parts of Speech

Indicate the part of speech of each italicized word or group of words by placing the appropriate abbreviations in the blanks.

n	noun	pro	pronoun
v	verb	adj	adjective
adv	adverb	conj	conjunction
prep	preposition		

_____ _____ 1. The *turtle* can be defined as a reptile *with* a shell.

_____ _____ 2. It is a *toothless* creature that can *smell* and see well.

_____ _____ 3. Some live *mostly* in the water, whereas others live mostly *in* places as dry as the desert.

_____ _____ 4. Both sea *and land* turtles will burrow and hibernate.

_____ _____ 5. Turtles are well known *for their* longevity.

_____ _____ 6. *Some live* to be more than a hundred years old.

_____ _____ 7. *Many* people purchase turtles for *pets*.

_____ _____ 8. Young turtles *eat chopped* raw meat, greens, fish, and worms.

_____ _____ 9. *They* need both sunlight *and* shade.

_____ _____ 10. *Some* people paint their *pet* turtles, a practice that can damage the turtles' shells.

_____ _____ 11. *Most* turtles are not *suitable* for pets.

_____ _____ 12. The snapping turtle *is* one such *species*.

_____ _____ 13. *It* can be *vicious* when cornered.

_____ _____ 14. The *common* snapper weighs up to sixty pounds and can snap off a set of fingers *with* one bite.

_____ _____ 15. Folklore holds that *when* a snapping turtle bites someone, it will not let go *until* it hears thunder.

_____ _____ 16. Stories *circulate* about a farmer who cut off the head of a snapping turtle that was biting someone, *yet*, even without its body, the snapper would not let go.

_____ _____ 17. The box turtle is a *gentle creature* and makes a good pet.

_____ _____ 18. It has a *hooked* beak, red eyes, and a splotchy *yellow* and brown shell.

_____ _____ 19. It eats worms, snails, berries, *and* other *fruit*.

_____ _____ 20. In the summer in the Midwest, one can *find* many box turtles crawling about, their solemn beaks red from a *meal* of blackberries.

2

Subjects and Verbs

The two crucial parts of any conventional sentence are the subject and the verb.

- The **subject** is who or what causes the action or expresses a state of being.
- The **verb** indicates what the subject is doing or is being.

The subject and verb often carry the meaning of the sentence. Consider this example:

<u>Mom</u> <u>left</u> for work.
subject verb

The subject *Mom* and the verb *left* indicate the basic content of the sentence while providing structure. So important are the subject and the verb that they alone are sufficient to create a complete sentence.

Jacob runs.

Grace thinks.

~ Subjects

The **simple subject** of a sentence is usually a single noun or pronoun.

The judge's <u>reputation</u> for order in the courtroom is well known.
simple subject

The **complete subject** is the simple subject with all its modifiers—that is, with all the words that describe or qualify it.

<u>The judge's reputation for order in the courtroom</u> is well known.
complete subject

To more easily identify simple subjects of sentences, you may want to review the following information about nouns and pronouns. (You may also want to review Chapter 1, "Parts of Speech.")

Nouns

Nouns are naming words. Nouns may name persons, animals, plants, places, things, substances, qualities, or ideas—for example, *Manny, armadillo, Atlanta, tree, rock, cloud, love, ghost, music,* and *virtue.*

Pronouns

A **pronoun** is a word that is used in place of a noun.

- Pronouns that can be used as subjects of sentences may represent specific persons or things and are called personal pronouns:

I	we
you	you
he, she, it	they

  EXAMPLE   <u>They</u> recommended my sister for the coaching position.
                  subject

- Indefinite pronouns refer to nouns (persons, places, things) in a general way:

each	everyone	nobody	somebody
either	neither	anyone	someone

  EXAMPLE   <u>Everyone</u> wants a copy of that photograph.
                 subject

- Other pronouns point out particular things:

  SINGULAR   *this, that*   PLURAL   *these, those*
              This is my treasure.   *These* are my jewels.
              That is your stuff.   *Those* are your trinkets.

- Still other pronouns introduce questions:

  Which is the best CD player?

  What are the main ingredients in a Twinkie?

  Who understands this computer command?

Caution: To be the subject of a sentence, a pronoun must stand alone.

     This is a treasure. (Subject is *this;* pronoun stands alone.)

     This *treasure* is mine. (Subject is *treasure. This* is an adjective—a word that describes a noun; *this* describes *treasure.*)

Compound Subjects

A subject may be **compound**; that is, it may consist of two or more subjects, usually joined by *and* or *or*, that function together.

> The *prosecutor* and the *attorney* for the defense made opening statements.
>
> *Luke* and his *friends* listened carefully.

Implied Subjects

A subject may be **implied** or understood. An imperative sentence—a sentence that gives a command—has *you* as the implied subject.

> (You) Sit in that chair, please.
>
> (You) Now take the oath.
>
> (You) Please read the notes carefully.

Trouble Spots

A **prepositional phrase** starts with a preposition (a word such as *at, in, of, to,* or *with*) and ends with one or more nouns or pronouns with their modifiers: *at the time, by the jury, in the courtroom, to the judge and the media, with controlled anger.* Some of the most common prepositions are the following:

about	before	but	into	past
above	behind	by	like	to
across	below	despite	near	toward
after	beneath	down	of	under
against	beside	for	off	until
among	between	from	on	upon
around	beyond	in	over	with

Some prepositions are composed of more than one word and are formed from other parts of speech:

according to	as far as	because of	in spite of
ahead of	as well as	in back of	instead of
along with	aside from	in front of	together with

Be careful not to confuse the subject of a sentence with the noun or pronoun (known as the **object of the preposition**) in a prepositional phrase. The object of a preposition (the final noun or pronoun of a prepositional phrase) cannot be the subject of a sentence.

The car with the dents is mine.
subject/prepositional phrase

The subject of the sentence is *car*. The word *dents* is the object of the preposition *with* and cannot be the subject of the sentence.

Most of the pie has been eaten.
subject/prepositional phrase

The person in the middle of the crowd has disappeared.
subject/prepositional phrase/prepositional phrase

The words *there* and *here* are adverbs (or filler words) and cannot be subjects.

There is no problem.
subject

Here is the issue.
subject

Exercise 1 Finding Subjects

Underline the simple or the compound subject, without modifiers.

EXAMPLE   A highly developed social structure and the use of bronze were marks of the Shang dynasty (about 1766 to 1122 BCE).

1. The earliest evidence of Chinese writing comes from that dynasty.

2. Archaeologists have found hundreds of animal bones and shells.

3. The bones and shells have written symbols on them.

4. These objects with writing on them are known as oracle bones.

5. Priests told fortunes with them.

6. Part of today's Chinese culture was developed 3,500 years ago.

7. In the Chinese method of writing, each character stands for an idea, not for a sound.

8. Some of the characters are very much like those in a modern Chinese newspaper.

9. They are not like Egyptian hieroglyphs.

10. Those Egyptian symbols stood for sounds in the spoken language.

11. In the Chinese language, there are practically no links between written and spoken forms.

12. Study your Chinese 101 textbook for more insights.

Exercise 2 Finding Subjects

Underline the simple or the compound subject, without modifiers.

1. Mahatma Gandhi gave his life for India and for peace.

2. Through a practice of nonviolent resistance, he led his people to freedom from the British.

3. Ponder his preference for behavior rather than accomplishment.

4. There was only good in his behavior and in his accomplishments.

5. His fasts, writings, and speeches inspired the people of India.

6. He taught his people self-sufficiency in weaving cloth and making salt for themselves against British law.

7. Gandhi urged the tolerance of all religions.

8. Finally, the British granted freedom to India.

9. Some leaders in India and a few foreign agitators questioned

   the freedom of religion.

10. Gandhi, the Indian prince of peace, was killed by an intolerant

   religious leader.

～ Verbs

Verbs show action or express being in relation to the subject of a sentence.

Types of Verbs

Action verbs show movement or accomplishment of an idea or a deed. Someone can *"consider* the statement" or *"hit* the ball." Here are other examples:

> Molina *left* the arena.
> Yuma *bought* the book.
> They *adopted* the child.
> Tao *understood* her main theories.

***Being* verbs** indicate existence. Few in number, they include *is, was, were, am,* and *are.*

> The movie *is* sad.
> The book *was* comprehensive.
> They *were* responsible.
> I *am* concerned.
> We *are* organized.

Verb Phrases

Verbs may occur as single words or as phrases. A **verb phrase** is made up of a main verb and one or more helping verbs such as the following:

is	was	can	have
are	were	could	had
am	will	would	has

Here are some sentences that contain verb phrases:

The judge *has presided* over many capital cases.

His rulings *are* seldom *overturned* on appeal.

I *should have known* the answer.

Compound Verbs

Verbs that are joined by a word such as *and* or *or* are called **compound verbs**.

The prosecutor *had presented* and *had won* famous cases.

Karla *prepared* carefully and *presented* her ideas with clarity.

We *will go* out for dinner or *skip* it entirely.

Compound verbs show two physical or mental actions performed by a simple or a compound subject.

Verbals

Do not confuse verbs with verbals. **Verbals** are verblike words in certain respects, but they function as other parts of speech. The three kinds of verbals are infinitives, gerunds, and participles.

An **infinitive** is made up of the word *to* and a verb. An infinitive provides information, but, unlike the true verb, it is not tied to the subject of the sentence. It acts as a noun or describing unit.

He wanted *to get* a bachelor's degree. (As an object of the verb *wanted*, *to get* acts as a noun and is an infinitive.)

A bachelor's degree is not easy *to obtain*. (As a modifier, or describer, of *easy*, *to obtain* acts as an adverb and is an infinitive.)

A **gerund** is a verblike word ending in *-ing* that acts as a noun.

Going to work was her main objective. (the activity of going to work)

She thought about *going* to work. (the act of going)

Going in each sentence acts as a noun. In the first sentence, it is the subject of the sentence. In the second, it is the object of the preposition *about*.

A **participle** is a verblike word that usually has an *-ing* or an *-ed* ending.

Walking to town in the dark, Luther lost his way.

Wanted by the FBI, Rachel was on the run.

In the first example, the word *walking* answers the question *When?* In the second, the word *wanted* answers the question *Which one?* Both *walking* and *wanted* are describing words; they are not the true verbs in the sentences.

Caution: Do not confuse verbals with true verbs. Verbals serve as nouns or modifiers. *Never*, *not*, and *hardly* are also modifiers, not verbs.

The attorney could *not* win the case without key witnesses. (*Not* is an adverb. The verb phrase is *could win*.)

The jury could *hardly* hear the witness. (*Hardly* is an adverb; *could hear* is the verb phrase.)

Exercise 3 Finding Verbs

Underline the verb(s) in each sentence.

1. Chimpanzees live and travel in social groups.

2. The composition of these groups varies in age and gender.

3. The habitat of the chimpanzees is mainly forests.

4. They spend more time in the trees than on the ground.

5. Each night they make a nest of branches and leaves in trees.

6. Sometimes a proud male will beat on his chest.

7. Chimpanzees are violent at times but usually live peacefully.

8. After finding food, a chimp hoots and shakes branches.

9. Other chimps hear the commotion and go to the food source.

10. Chimp tools, such as leaf sponges and sticks, are primitive.

Exercise 4   Finding Verbs

Underline the verb(s) in each sentence.

1. Chimpanzees share many features with human beings.

2. More than 90 percent of basic genetic make-up is shared.

3. Both human beings and chimps can use reason.

4. Chimps have a remarkable talent for communication.

5. Chimps do not have the capacity for human speech.

6. However, chimps can use other symbols.

7. In one experiment, chimps learned American Sign Language.

8. Chimps can learn a complex system of language.

9. Chimp scholar Washoe learned more than 160 signs and could

    ask questions.

10. Another chimp, Lana, uses a computer.

Exercise 5   Finding Subjects and Verbs

*Circle the subject(s) and underline the verb(s) in the following
sentences. You will have to supply the subject for one sentence.*

1. Read this exercise carefully.

2. What causes earthquakes?

3. How much damage can they do?

4. Earthquakes shake the earth.

5. There is no simple answer to the question of cause.

6. The earth is covered by rock plates.

7. Instead of merely covering, they are in constant motion.

8. These plates bump into each other and then pass over each other.

9. The rocks are squeezed and stretched.

10. They pull apart or pile up and cause breaks in the earth's surface.

11. These breaks are called *faults*.

12. The formation of a fault is an earthquake.

13. During the breaking or shifting, a seismic wave travels across the earth's surface.

14. These quaking vibrations are especially destructive near the point of the breaking or shifting.

15. Their force is equal to as much as ten thousand times that of an atomic bomb.

16. For many years, scientists have tried to predict earthquakes.

17. There has been little success in their endeavors.

18. Earthquakes are identified only after the fact.

19. Some states, such as California, experience many earthquakes.

20. Somewhere in the earth, a quake of some magnitude is almost certainly occurring now.

⌒ Location of Subjects and Verbs

Although the subject *usually* appears before the verb, it may follow
the verb instead:

Into the court <u>stumbled</u> the <u>defendant</u>.
verb subject

From tiny acorns <u>grow</u> mighty <u>oaks</u>.
verb subject

There <u>was</u> little <u>support</u> for him in the audience.
verb subject

Here <u>are</u> your <u>books</u> and your <u>papers</u>.
verb subject subject

Verb phrases are often broken up in a question. Do not overlook
a part of the verb that is separated from another in a question such
as "Where had the defendant gone on that fateful night?" If you have
trouble finding the verb phrase, recast the question, making it into
a statement: "The defendant *had gone* where on that fateful night."
The result will not necessarily be a smooth or complete statement,
but you will be able to see the basic elements more easily.

Can the defense lawyer control the direction of the trial?

Change the question to a statement to find the verb phrase:

The defense lawyer *can control* the direction of the trial.

⌒ Chapter Review

Exercise 6   Finding Subjects and Verbs

Circle the subject(s) and underline the verb(s) in the following sen-
tences. You will have to supply the subject for one sentence.

1. Consider this information about Puerto Rico.

2. Just where is Puerto Rico?

3. What do the words *Puerto Rico* mean?

4. Are Puerto Ricans U.S. citizens?

5. How is Puerto Rico different from our states?

6. Will it ever become a state?

7. The Commonwealth of Puerto Rico is located southeast of Florida.

8. *Puerto Rico* means "rich port."

9. Puerto Rico became a U.S. territory in 1898 after the Spanish-American War.

10. It became a commonwealth with its own constitution in 1952.

11. Puerto Ricans are citizens of the United States.

12. They cannot vote in presidential elections and do not pay federal income taxes.

13. On several occasions, they have voted not to become a state.

14. However, there are many in favor of statehood.

15. The majority of the citizens speak Spanish.

16. Their economy is based on manufacturing, fishing, and agriculture.

17. The Caribbean National Forest is treasured by Puerto Ricans and visitors.

18. In this tropical rain forest, parrots and orchids can be seen.

19. Tourists by the thousands visit the Phosphorescent Bay at La Parguera.

20. On moonless nights, the phosphorescent plankton light the water.

Exercise 7   Finding Subjects and Verbs

Circle the simple or the compound subject(s) and underline the verb(s) in the following sentences. You will have to supply the subject for one sentence.

1. Read this exercise and learn about the Aztec empire in Mexico.

2. Aztec cities were as large as those in Europe at that time.

3. Government and religion were important concerns.

4. There was little difference between the two institutions.

5. They built huge temples to their gods and sacrificed human beings.

6. The religious ceremonies related mainly to their concerns about plentiful harvests.

7. Aztec society had nobles, commoners, serfs, and slaves.

8. The family included a husband, a wife, children, and some relatives of the husband.

9. At the age of ten, boys went to school and girls either went to school or learned domestic skills at home.

10. The Aztecs wore loose-fitting garments, they lived in adobe houses, and they ate tortillas.

11. Scholars in this culture developed a calendar of 365 days.

12. Huge Aztec calendars of stone are now in museums.

13. The Aztec language was similar to that of the Comanche and Pima Indians.

14. The Aztec written language was pictographic and represented ideas and sounds.

15. Both religion and government required young men to pursue warfare.

16. By pursuing warfare, the soldiers could capture others for slaves and sacrifice, and they could enlarge the Aztec empire.

17. In 1519, Hernando Cortez landed in Mexico.

18. He was joined by native people other than Aztecs.

19. After first welcoming Cortez and his army, the Aztecs then rebelled.

20. The Spaniards killed Emperor Montezuma II, and then they defeated the Aztecs.

Exercise 8 Writing Sentences with Subjects and Verbs

Using the topic of work, *write five sentences. Circle the simple or the compound subject(s) and underline the verb(s).*

1. _____

_____

_____

_____

_____

2. _____

_____

_____

_____

_____

3. _____

_____

_____

_____

_____

4. _____

_____

_____

_____

_____

5. _____

_____

_____

_____

_____

3

Kinds of Sentences

The four kinds of basic sentences in English are simple, compound, complex, and compound-complex. The terms may be new to you, but if you can recognize subjects and verbs, with a little instruction and practice you should be able to identify and write any of the four kinds of sentences. The only new idea to master is the concept of the *clause*.

~ Clauses

A **clause** is a group of words with a subject and a verb that functions as a part or all of a complete sentence. There are two kinds of clauses: independent (main) and dependent (subordinate).

> INDEPENDENT CLAUSE   I have the money.
>
> DEPENDENT CLAUSE   When I have the money

Independent Clauses

An **independent (main) clause** is a group of words with a subject and a verb that can stand alone and make sense. An independent clause expresses a complete thought by itself and can be written as a separate sentence.

> Avita plays the bass guitar.
>
> The manager is not at fault.

Dependent Clauses

A **dependent clause** is a group of words with a subject and a verb that depends on a main clause to give it meaning.

> since Helen came home (no meaning alone)
>
> <u>Since Helen came home,</u> <u>her mother has been happy.</u> (has meaning)
>   dependent clause   independent clause

27

because she was needed (no meaning alone)

<u>She stayed in the game</u> <u>because she was needed.</u> (has meaning)
    independent clause   dependent clause

Dependent clauses are connected to the rest of the sentence by subordinating conjunctions such as the following:

after	if	until
although	in order that	when
as	provided that	whenever
as if	rather than	where
because	since	whereas
before	so that	wherever
even if	than	whether
even though	unless	while

Relative Clauses

A **relative clause**, one type of dependent clause, begins with a relative pronoun, a pronoun such as *that, which,* or *who.* Relative pronouns *relate* the clause to another word in the sentence.

that fell last night (no meaning alone)

The snow <u>that fell last night</u> is nearly gone. (has meaning)
            dependent clause

In the sentence above, the relative pronoun *that* relates the dependent clause to the subject of the sentence, *snow.*

who stayed in the game (no meaning alone)

<u>She was the only one</u> <u>who stayed in the game.</u>
    independent clause   dependent clause

In the sentence above, the relative pronoun *who* relates the dependent clause to the word *one.*

⌒ Trouble Spot: Phrases

A **phrase** is a group of words that go together. It differs from a clause in that a phrase does not have a subject and a verb. So far, we have seen prepositional phrases (*in the house, beyond the horizon*) and verbal phrases (infinitive phrase: *to go home*; participial phrase: *disconnected from the printer*; and gerund phrase: *running the computer*).

Exercise 1 Identifying Clauses and Phrases

Identify the following groups of words as an independent, or a main, clause (has a subject and verb and can stand alone); a dependent clause (has a subject and verb but cannot stand alone); or a phrase (a group of words that go together but do not have a subject and a verb).

_____ 1. Under the table

_____ 2. After I won the lottery

_____ 3. I won the lottery

_____ 4. To find a fossil

_____ 5. Fred found a fossil

_____ 6. Over the bridge and through the woods

_____ 7. We chased the wind over the bridge and through the woods

_____ 8. Because it rated highly

_____ 9. Find matching socks

_____ 10. Because of the new guidelines

∼ Types of Sentences

The following discussion covers sentence types according to this principle: On the basis of the number and kinds of clauses it contains, a sentence may be classified as simple, compound, complex, or compound-complex.

Type	Definition	Example
Simple	One independent clause	She did the work well.
Compound	Two or more independent clauses	She did the work well, and she was paid well.
Complex	One independent clause (underlined) and one or more dependent clauses (italicized)	*Because she did the work well*, she was paid well.
Compound-Complex	Two or more independent clauses (underlined) and one or more dependent clauses (italicized)	*Because she did the work well*, she was paid well, and she was satisfied.

Simple Sentences

A **simple sentence** consists of one independent clause and no dependent clauses. It may contain phrases and have more than one subject or verb.

> The *lake looks* beautiful in the moonlight. (one subject and one verb)
>
> The *Army, Navy,* and *Marines sent* troops to the disaster area. (three subjects and one verb)
>
> *We sang* the old songs and *danced* happily at their wedding. (one subject and two verbs)
>
> My *father, mother,* and *sister came* to the school play, *applauded* the performers, and *attended* the party afterward. (three subjects and three verbs)

Exercise 2   Writing Simple Sentences

Write six simple sentences. The first five have been started for you.

1. This school _____

2. My desk _____

3. My friend _____

4. In the evening, I _____

5. Last night, the _____

6. _____

Compound Sentences

A **compound sentence** consists of two or more independent clauses with no dependent clauses. Take, for example, the following two independent clauses:

> He opened the door. He found the missing paper.

Here are three ways to join the independent clauses to form a compound sentence.

1. Connect the two independent clauses using a connecting word called a **coordinating conjunction**. The coordinating

conjunctions are *for, and, nor, but, or, yet, so.* Remember the acronym FANBOYS.

He opened the door, *and* he found the missing paper.

He opened the door, *so* he found the missing paper.

Use a comma before the coordinating conjunction between two independent clauses (unless one of the clauses is extremely short).

2. Put a semicolon between the clauses.

He opened the door; he found the missing paper.

3. Use a transitional word, such as *however* or *therefore.* Place a semicolon before the word and a comma after.

He found the missing paper; *therefore,* he was satisfied.

Exercise 3 Writing Compound Sentences

Write five compound sentences using coordinating conjunctions. The sentences have been started for you. Then write the same five compound sentences without the coordinating conjunctions. Use a semicolon to join the independent clauses, and, if appropriate, include transitional words such as therefore *and* however.

1. He played well in the first quarter, but he _____

2. She was happy for a while, and then _____

3. The dog is our best friend, for _____

4. She is not the best player, nor is _____

5. I will try to help, but _____

6. _____

7. _____

8. _____

9. _____

10. _____

Complex Sentences

A **complex sentence** consists of one independent clause and one or more dependent clauses. In the following sentences, the dependent clauses are italicized.

> *When lilacs are in bloom,* we love to visit friends in the country. (one dependent clause and one independent clause)
>
> *Although it rained last night,* we decided to take the path *that led through the woods.* (one independent clause and two dependent clauses)

A relative clause (see page 28) can be the dependent clause in a complex sentence.

> I knew the actress *who played that part in the 1980s.*

Punctuation tip: Use a comma after a dependent clause that appears before the main clause.

> *When the bus arrived,* we quickly boarded.

Exercise 4   Writing Complex Sentences

Write six complex sentences. The first five have been started for you.

1. Although he did the work quickly, _____

2. _____ because the storm hit.

3. After you go to the party, _____

4. Because you are smart, _____

5. _____ when he turned to leave.

6. _____

Compound-Complex Sentences

A **compound-complex sentence** consists of two or more independent clauses and one or more dependent clauses.

> COMPOUND-
> COMPLEX   Albert enlisted in the Army, and Robert, who
> SENTENCE   was his older brother, joined him a day later.

| INDEPENDENT CLAUSES | Albert enlisted in the Army |
| | Robert joined him a day later |

| DEPENDENT CLAUSE | who was his older brother |

| COMPOUND-COMPLEX SENTENCE | Because Mr. Roberts was a talented teacher, he was voted Teacher of the Year, and his students prospered. |

| INDEPENDENT CLAUSES | he was voted Teacher of the Year |
| | his students prospered |

| DEPENDENT CLAUSE | Because Mr. Roberts was a talented teacher |

Exercise 5 Writing Compound-Complex Sentences

Write six compound-complex sentences. The first five have been started for you.

1. Because he was my friend, I had to defend him, and I _____

   _____

2. Although he started late, he finished rapidly, and he _____

   _____

3. She had not eaten since the clock struck twelve, and she _____

   _____

4. We didn't realize that he was sick, but _____

   _____

5. If you want to leave, _____

   _____

6. _____

   _____

∼ Chapter Review

Exercise 6   Identifying Types of Sentences

Indicate the kind of sentence by writing the appropriate letter(s) in the blank.

S   simple
CP   compound
CX   complex
CC   compound-complex

_____   1. The most popular sport in the world is soccer.

_____   2. People in ancient China and Japan had a form of soccer, and even Rome had a game that resembled soccer.

_____   3. The game as it is played today got its start in England.

_____   4. In the Middle Ages, whole towns played soccer on Shrove Tuesday.

_____   5. Goals were built at opposite ends of town, and hundreds of people who lived in those towns would play on each side.

_____   6. Such games resembled full-scale brawls.

_____   7. The first side to score a goal won and was declared village champion.

_____   8. Then both sides tended to the wounded, and they didn't play again for a whole year.

_____   9. The rules of the game were written in the late 1800s at British boarding schools.

_____   10. Now nearly every European country has a national soccer team, and the teams participate in international tournaments.

Exercise 7 Identifying Types of Sentences

Indicate the kind of sentence by writing the appropriate letter(s) in the blank.

S   simple
CP   compound
CX   complex
CC   compound-complex

_____   1. Leonardo da Vinci was one of the greatest painters of the Italian Renaissance.

_____   2. His portrait *Mona Lisa* and his religious scene *The Last Supper* rank among the most famous pictures ever painted.

_____   3. Da Vinci was trained to be a painter, but he was also one of the most versatile geniuses in all of history.

_____   4. His interests and achievements spread into an astonishing variety of fields that are usually considered scientific specialties.

_____   5. Da Vinci studied anatomy, astronomy, botany, and geology, and he designed machines and drew plans for hundreds of inventions.

_____   6. He recorded his scientific observations and his ideas for inventions in notebooks.

_____   7. About 4,200 pages still exist; they are filled with brilliant drawings that reveal da Vinci's powers of observation and skill as a draftsman.

_____   8. His recorded ideas were ahead of their time; for example, he drew plans for a flying machine, and he came up with the parachute, too.

_____   9. These drawings rank among da Vinci's greatest masterpieces.

_____   10. Although scientists of his day believed in an Earth-centered universe, da Vinci's notebooks reveal his understanding of the Earth's movement around the Sun.

Exercise 8   Identifying Types of Sentences

Indicate the kind of sentence by writing the appropriate letter(s) in the blank.

S   simple
CP   compound
CX   complex
CC   compound-complex

_____ 1. Around 500 BCE, the Mayans began to create their civilization in the southern Gulf Coast region and present-day Guatemala.

_____ 2. The result was remarkable for its brilliant achievements.

_____ 3. Although they had no wheeled vehicles and no beasts of burden such as horses or oxen, they moved great pieces of stone to build their temples.

_____ 4. They had no iron tools; however, because they shaped their stone blocks so skillfully, their pyramids still stand.

_____ 5. The pyramids were the center of Mayan religious ceremonies.

_____ 6. The Mayans built many city-states, and the ruins of at least eighty have been found.

_____ 7. The tallest pyramid was as high as a twenty-story building.

_____ 8. A small temple was constructed at the top, where priests conducted ceremonies.

_____ 9. These pyramids were surrounded by plazas and avenues.

_____ 10. The Mayans were able to build complex structures and to invent an accurate calendar because they knew mathematics well.

4

Combining Sentences, Avoiding Omissions, and Achieving Sentence Variety

The simple sentence, the most basic sentence in the English language, can be exceptionally useful and powerful. Some of the greatest statements in literature have been presented in the simple sentence. Its strength is in its singleness of purpose. However, a piece of writing made up of a long series of simple sentences is likely to be monotonous. Moreover, the form may suggest a separateness of ideas that does not serve your purpose well. If your ideas are closely related, some equal in importance and some not, you can combine sentences to show the relationships between your ideas.

If you combine sentences skillfully, you will avoid omissions and achieve a variety of sentence patterns.

Coordination: The Compound Sentence

If you intend to communicate two equally important and closely related ideas, you certainly will want to place them close together, probably in a compound sentence.

Suppose we take two simple sentences that we want to combine:

I am very tired. I worked very hard today.

We have already looked at coordinating conjunctions as a way of joining independent clauses to create compound sentences. Depending on which coordinating conjunction you use, you can show different kinds of relationships. (The following list is arranged according to the FANBOYS acronym. Only the first conjunction joins the original two sentences.)

For shows a reason:

I am very tired, *for* I worked very hard today.

37

And shows equal ideas:

I am very tired, *and* I want to rest for a few minutes.

Nor indicates a negative choice or alternative:

I am not tired, *nor* am I hungry right now.

But shows contrast:

I am very tired, *but* I have no time to rest now.

Or indicates a choice or an alternative:

I will take a nap, *or* I will go out jogging.

Yet indicates contrast:

I am very tired, *yet* I am unable to relax.

So points to a result:

I am very tired, *so* I will take a nap.

Punctuation with Coordinating Conjunctions

When you combine two sentences by using a coordinating conjunction, drop the period, change the capital letter to a small letter, and insert a comma before the coordinating conjunction.

$$
\text{Independent clause}
\left\{
\begin{array}{l}
, \textit{for} \\
, \textit{and} \\
, \textit{nor} \\
, \textit{but} \\
, \textit{or} \\
, \textit{yet} \\
, \textit{so}
\end{array}
\right\}
\text{independent clause.}
$$

Exercise 1 Combining Sentences: Compound

Combine the following pairs of sentences by deleting the first period, changing the capital letter that begins the second sentence to a small letter, and inserting a comma and an appropriate coordinating conjunction from the FANBOYS list. Feel free to reword the sentences as necessary.

1. James Francis "Jim" Thorpe, a Sac and Fox Indian, was born in 1888 near Prague, Oklahoma. At the age of sixteen, he left home to enroll in the Carlisle Indian School in Pennsylvania.

2. He had had little experience playing football. He led his small college to victories against championship teams.

3. He had scarcely heard of other sports. He golfed in the 70s, bowled above 200, and played varsity basketball and lacrosse.

4. In the 1912 Olympic Games for amateur athletes at Stockholm, Jim Thorpe entered the two most rigorous events, the decathlon and the pentathlon. He won both.

5. King Gustav V of Sweden told him, "You, Sir, are the greatest athlete in the world." Jim Thorpe said, "Thanks, King."

6. Later it was said he had once been paid fifteen dollars a week to play baseball, making him a professional athlete. The Olympic medals were taken from him.

7. Soon a Major League baseball scout did offer Thorpe a respectable contract. He played in the National League for six seasons.

8. Not content to play only one sport, he also earned a good salary for that time in professional football. After competing for fifteen years, he said he had never played for the money.

9. Many regard Jim Thorpe as the greatest athlete of the twentieth century. He excelled in many sports at the highest levels of athletic competition.

10. Off the playing fields, he was known by his friends as a modest, quiet man. On the fields, he was a person of joyful combat.

Semicolons and Conjunctive Adverbs

We have also already looked at using a semicolon to join independent clauses to make a compound sentence. Here are two more simple sentences to combine:

> We were late. We missed the first act.

We can make one compound sentence using these simple sentences by joining the two clauses with a semicolon:

> We were late; we missed the first act.

We can also use words called conjunctive adverbs after semicolons to make the relationship between the two clauses clearer. Look at how the conjunctive adverb *therefore* adds the idea of "as a result."

> We were late; *therefore*, we missed the first act.

Conjunctive adverbs include the following words and phrases: *also, consequently, furthermore, hence, however, in fact, moreover, nevertheless, now, on the other hand, otherwise, soon, therefore, similarly, then, thus.*

When you coordinate ideas with conjunctive adverbs, consider the meanings of these words:

> As a result of: *therefore, consequently, hence, thus, then*
> To the contrary or with reservation: *however, nevertheless, otherwise, on the other hand*
> In addition to: *moreover, also*
> To emphasize or specify: *in fact, for example*
> To compare: *similarly*

Punctuation with Semicolons and Conjunctive Adverbs

When you combine two sentences by using a semicolon, replace the period with a semicolon and change the capital letter that begins the second sentence to a small letter. If you wish to use a conjunctive adverb, insert it after the semicolon and usually put a comma after it. (However, usually no comma follows *then, now, thus,* and *soon.*) The first letters of ten common, though there are other, conjunctive adverbs make up the acronym HOTSHOT CAT.

$$
\text{Independent clause}
\left\{
\begin{array}{l}
\text{; however,} \\
\text{; otherwise,} \\
\text{; therefore,} \\
\text{; similarly,} \\
\text{; hence} \\
\text{; on the other hand,} \\
\text{; then} \\
\text{; consequently,} \\
\text{; also,} \\
\text{; thus}
\end{array}
\right\}
\text{independent clause.}
$$

Exercise 2   Combining Sentences: Compound

Combine the following pairs of sentences by replacing the first period with a semicolon, changing the capital letter that begins the second sentence to a small letter, and inserting a conjunctive adverb if appropriate. Consider the list of conjunctive adverbs (HOTSHOT CAT and others). Do not use a conjunctive adverb in every sentence.

1. The legendary island of Atlantis has fascinated people for centuries. It probably never existed.

2. According to the Greek writer Plato, the people of Atlantis were very ambitious and warlike. They planned to conquer all of the Mediterranean.

3. Initially, they were successful in subduing areas to the west. They became wealthy.

4. Then the people of Atlantis became proud. They became corrupt and wicked.

5. They were confident and attacked Athens. Athens and its allies defeated the invaders.

6. The story of Atlantis is probably just a tale. Many people have believed it.

7. Some writers have tried to link the legend with such real places as America and the Canary Islands. No link has been found.

8. The Minoan civilization on Crete was destroyed by tidal waves. A similar fate may have befallen Atlantis.

9. Some people speculate about a volcanic explosion on Atlantis. A volcanic eruption did destroy part of the island Thera in the Eastern Mediterranean in 1500 BCE.

10. Some writers have conjectured that American Indians migrated to the New World by way of Atlantis. Archaeologists dispute that idea.

⁓ Subordination: The Complex Sentence

Whereas a compound sentence contains independent clauses that are equally important and closely related, a complex sentence combines ideas of unequal value. The following two sentences can be combined as either a compound sentence or a complex sentence, depending on whether the writer thinks the ideas are of equal value.

My neighbors are considerate. They never play loud music.

Combined as a compound sentence, suggesting that the ideas are of equal value, the new sentence looks like this:

<u>My neighbors are considerate</u>, and <u>they never play loud music</u>.
independent clause   independent clause
(main idea)   (main idea)

Here are the same two ideas combined as a complex sentence, suggesting that the ideas are of unequal value:

<u>Because my neighbors are considerate,</u> <u>they never play loud music.</u>

dependent clause   independent clause

(less important idea)   (main idea)

Although both the compound and complex forms are correct, the complex form conveys the ideas more precisely in this sentence because one idea does seem to be more important—one idea depends on the other.

Thus if you have two sentences with closely related ideas and one is clearly more important than the other, consider combining them in a complex sentence. Compare these two paragraphs:

- Version 1 contains six simple sentences, implying that the ideas are of equal value:

  (1) I was very upset. (2) The Fourth of July fireworks were especially loud. (3) My dog ran away. (4) The animal control officer made his morning rounds. (5) He found my dog in another part of town. (6) I was relieved.

- Version 2 consists of two simple sentences and two complex sentences, showing that some ideas are more important than others:

  (1) I was very upset. (2) Because the Fourth of July fireworks were especially loud, my dog ran away. (3) When the animal control officer made his morning rounds, he found my dog in another part of town. (4) I was relieved.

You will probably consider Version 2 superior to Version 1. Sentences 2 and 3 are closely related, but 3 is more important. And sentences 4 and 5 are closely related, but 5 is more important. The revision made each pair into a complex sentence.

Although you could combine sentences 1 and 2, the result would be illogical because the wrong idea would be conveyed:

I was very upset because the Fourth of July fireworks were especially loud.

The person was very upset because the dog ran away, not because the fireworks were especially loud.

As you learned in Chapter 3, a complex sentence is composed of one independent clause and one or more dependent clauses. In combining two independent clauses to write a complex sentence, your first step is to decide on a word that will best show the relationship between the clauses. Words that show the relationship of a dependent clause to an independent one are called subordinating conjunctions. The italicized words in the sentences that follow are subordinating conjunctions. Consider the meaning as well as the placement of each one.

> *Because* the storm hit, the game was canceled.
>
> *After* the storm passed, the clown dogs began to bark.
>
> *When* she read her poem, they were moved to fits of hysterics.
>
> He did not volunteer to work on the holiday, *although* the pay was good.
>
> No one has visited her *since* she moved into town.
>
> They decided to wait *until* the cows came home.
>
> They refused to work *unless* they were allowed to wear chef's hats.
>
> *Before* the session ended, all the "hep cats" blew some sweet sounds.

Other subordinating conjunctions include the following:

as	if	so that	whereas
as if	in order that	than	wherever
even if	provided that	whenever	whether
even though	rather than	where	while

Punctuation with Subordinating Conjunctions

If the dependent clause comes *before* the main clause, set it off with a comma.

> Before you dive, be sure there is water in the pool.

If the dependent clause comes *after* or *within* the main clause, set it off only if the clause is not necessary to the meaning of the main clause or if the dependent clause begins with the word *although* or *though*.

> Be sure there is water in the pool *before* you dive.
>
> We went home *after* the concert had ended.
>
> Yogi continued to brush, *although* he had painted the cabinet twice.

You have already learned that a relative clause—one that starts with a relative pronoun like *that, which,* or *who*—can be the dependent clause in a sentence. If we look at the two sentences we started with, we can see how they can be combined using a relative clause.

> My neighbors are considerate. They never play loud music.

Combined as a complex sentence with a relative clause as the dependent clause, the new sentence looks like this:

> My neighbors, <u>who are considerate</u>, never play loud music.
>   dependent clause

Punctuation with Relative Pronouns

Set the dependent clause off with commas when it is not necessary to the sentence. Do not set the clause off if it is necessary for the meaning of the sentence.

> Everyone *who tries* will pass this class. (The dependent clause is necessary because one would not say, "Everyone will pass this class.")
>
> Kumar, *who tries*, will pass this class. (The dependent clause is not necessary because one can say, "Kumar will pass this class.")

The relative pronoun *which* usually refers to things. The word *which* almost always indicates that a clause is not necessary for the meaning of the sentence. Therefore, a clause beginning with *which* is almost always set off by commas.

> My car, *which is ten years old*, has a flat tire.

The relative pronoun *that* also usually refers to things. However, the word *that* almost always indicates that the clause *is* necessary for the meaning of the sentence. Therefore, a clause beginning with *that* is *not* set off by commas.

> The car *that* has a flat tire is ten years old.

The relative pronouns *who* and *whom*, as well as *whoever* and *whomever*, usually refer to people. Clauses that begin with those relative pronouns are not set off by commas if they are necessary for the meaning of the sentence; if they are not necessary, they are set off.

> A person *who* has a way with words is often quoted. (necessary for the meaning of the sentence)
>
> My uncle, *whom* I quote often, has a way with words. (not necessary for the meaning of the sentence)

Exercise 3   Combining Sentences: Complex

Combine the following pairs of sentences into one complex sentence. Insert an appropriate subordinating conjunction or relative pronoun, add or fix punctuation, and make other minor changes as needed. Sentences that should be combined by using a relative pronoun are indicated.

1. (relative pronoun) Frida Kahlo is known as one of the great painters of the twentieth century. She was born in 1907 in Coyoacan, Mexico.

2. She claimed to have been born in 1910. She wanted to have her birth associated with the Mexican Revolution.

3. (relative pronoun) She was born and died in the same house. The house was called *La Casa Azul* or "The Blue House."

4. Frida's father, Guillermo, was born in Germany. Her mother, Matilde, lived her entire life in Mexico.

5. Frida experienced much physical pain in her life. She contracted polio at age six and years later was badly injured in a bus accident.

6. The accident happened. Frida was bedridden in extreme pain for months at a time on a number of occasions.

7. She started painting. She was in a body cast following the accident.

8. (relative pronoun) Eventually she married the famous Mexican muralist, Diego Rivera. He critiqued her paintings and gave her encouragement.

9. Her paintings include many self-portraits. She painted other subjects, as well.

10. (relative pronoun) Many art lovers have become enchanted by her powerful and haunting paintings. These paintings often include symbolic imagery from indigenous Amerindian culture.

∼ Coordination and Subordination: The Compound-Complex Sentence

At times, you may want to show the relationship of three or more ideas within one sentence. If that relationship involves two or more main ideas and one or more supporting ideas, the combination can be stated in a compound-complex sentence (two or more independent clauses and one or more dependent clauses).

> Before Carson learned how to operate a computer,
> dependent clause
>
> he had trouble with his typewritten assignments,
> independent clause
>
> but now he produces clean, attractive material.
> independent clause

In our discussion of the complex sentence, we presented this group of six sentences:

> I was very upset. The Fourth of July fireworks were especially loud. My dog ran away. The animal control officer made his morning rounds. He found my dog in another part of town. I was relieved.

We then converted the group of six sentences to four:

> I was very upset. Because the Fourth of July fireworks were especially loud, my dog ran away. When the animal control officer made his morning rounds, he found my dog in another part of town. I was relieved.

If we wanted to show an even closer relationship of ideas, we could combine the two complex sentences in this way (the italicized sentence is compound-complex):

> I was very upset. *Because the Fourth of July fireworks were especially loud, my dog ran away; but when the animal control*

officer made his morning rounds, he found my dog in another part of town. I was relieved.

Punctuation of Complicated Compound or Compound-Complex Sentences

If a compound or compound-complex sentence has one or more commas in the first clause, you may want to use a semicolon before the coordinating conjunction between the two clauses. Its purpose is to show the reader very clearly the division between the two independent clauses. The preceding example illustrates this use of the semicolon.

Exercise 4   Combining Sentences: Compound-Complex

Combine each group of sentences into one compound-complex sentence. Use the rules of sentence combining and punctuation discussed in this chapter.

1. Helen Keller suffered a serious childhood illness. She became blind and deaf. At first her parents did not know what to do.

2. Her parents would not give up despite discouraging advice. They advertised for a teacher. A tutor named Anne Sullivan agreed to help.

3. Young Helen began to discover the world through her sense of touch. She learned the alphabet. She started connecting words with objects.

4. Her physical condition was irreversible. Her progress was rapid. In three years she could read Braille.

5. She could not talk. She used sign language for speech. She used a special typewriter to write.

6. She reached the age of ten. She took speech lessons from a teacher of the deaf. In six years she could speak well enough to be understood.

7. She attended college. She still needed help. Anne Sullivan continued as her tutor and interpreter.

8. She graduated from college with honors. She became involved in programs to help the deaf and blind communicate. She wrote books and articles about problems of the disabled.

9. The effects of World War II presented special problems. Helen Keller helped disabled people in other countries. She helped soldiers blinded in the war.

10. Helen Keller died in 1968. She had an international reputation as a humanitarian. Her books had been translated into more than fifty languages.

～ Other Ways to Combine Ideas

In this chapter you have learned how to combine simple sentences into compound, complex, and compound-complex sentences that show the coordination and subordination of ideas. There are other methods of combining ideas. Here are four you may want to use in your own writing:

1. Use an **appositive**, which is a noun or a noun phrase that immediately follows a noun or pronoun and renames it.

   Susan is the leading scorer on the team. Susan is a quick and strong player.

   Susan, *a quick and strong player*, is the leading scorer on the team.

2. Use a **prepositional phrase**, a preposition followed by a noun or pronoun object.

> Dolly Parton wrote a song about a coat. The coat had many colors.
>
> Dolly Parton wrote a song about a coat *of many colors.*

3. Drop the subject in the sentence that follows, and combine the sentences.

> Some items are too damaged for recycling. They must be disposed of.
>
> Some items are too damaged for recycling *and* must be disposed of.

4. Use a **participial phrase**, a group of words that includes a participle, which is a verbal that usually ends in *-ing* or *-ed*.

> Miguel rowed smoothly. He reached the shore.
>
> *Rowing smoothly,* Miguel reached the shore.

〰 Omissions: When Parts Are Missing

The omission of a word or words may occur during sentence combining. Do not omit words that are needed to make your sentences clear and logical. Of the many types of undesirable construction in which necessary words are omitted, the following are the most common:

1. **Subjects.** Do not omit a necessary subject in a sentence with two verbs.

ILLOGICAL	The cost of the car was $12,000 but would easily last me through college. (subject of *last*)
LOGICAL	The cost of the car was $12,000, but the car would easily last me through college.

2. **Verbs.** Do not omit verbs that are needed because of a change in the number of the subject or a change of tense.

ILLOGICAL	The bushes were trimmed and the grass mowed. (verb of *grass*)
LOGICAL	The bushes were trimmed and the grass was mowed.

ILLOGICAL   True honesty always has and always will be
admired by most people. (tense)

LOGICAL   True honesty always has been and always will
be admired by most people.

3. ***That* as a conjunction.** The conjunction *that* should not be
omitted from a dependent clause if there is danger of misread-
ing the sentence.

MISLEADING   We believed Marcos, if not stopped, would hurt
himself. (*that* after *believed*)

CLEAR   We believed that Marcos, if not stopped, would
hurt himself.

4. **Prepositions.** Do not omit prepositions in idiomatic phrases, in
expressions of time, and in parallel phrases.

ILLOGICAL   Weekends the campus is deserted. (time)

LOGICAL   During weekends the campus is deserted.

ILLOGICAL   I have neither love nor patience with untrained
dogs. (parallel phrases)

LOGICAL   I have neither love for nor patience with
untrained dogs.

ILLOGICAL   Macarena's illness was something we heard only
after her recovery. (*about* after *heard*)

LOGICAL   Macarena's illness was something we heard
about only after her recovery.

Exercise 5   Correcting Omissions

*Identify the kinds of omissions by writing one of the following
words in the blank to the left:* subject, verb, conjunction, preposition. *Insert the necessary words in the sentences.*

_____   1. The Golden Gate Bridge was completed in
1937 and today considered one of the most
beautiful bridges in the world.

_____   2. Few know when the bridge was proposed many were against its construction for safety reasons.

_____   3. The bridge spans the opening to San Francisco Bay known as the Golden Gate, is made of steel.

_____   4. The Golden Gate Bridge spans 1.7 miles over deep water and 746 feet tall.

_____   5. Many days the bridge is buffeted by high winds and obscured by fog.

_____   6. Before there was a bridge, ferry boats were owned by a railroad company joined Marin County with San Francisco.

_____   7. Charles Alton Ellis was a major contributor to the design of the bridge virtually unknown until years later.

_____   8. The bridge received its final orange color, the navy wanted it to be painted black with yellow stripes for visibility.

_____   9. On television and the movies, the bridge often exists as a romantic backdrop.

_____   10. The Golden Gate Bridge has been recognized as one of the Wonders of the Modern World, and will continue to be amazed by it for years to come.

∿ Variety in Sentences: Types, Order, Length, Beginnings

Sentences can be written in a variety of ways to achieve freshness and clarity. Much of this polishing takes place during revision, and often during sentence combining. Here are a few techniques for the main variations.

Types

You have learned that all four types of sentences are sound. Your task as a writer is to decide which one to use for a particular thought.

That decision may not be made until you revise your composition. Then you can choose on the basis of the relationship of ideas:

> **Simple:** a single idea
> **Compound:** two closely related ideas
> **Complex:** one idea more important than the other
> **Compound-complex:** a combination of the two parts

These types were all covered in Chapter 3. This chapter provides further practice, as you combine sentences.

Order

You will choose the order of parts and information according to what you want to emphasize. Typically the most emphatic location is at the end of any unit.

Length

Uncluttered and direct, short sentences commonly draw attention. Because that focus occurs only when short sentences stand out from longer sentences, you would usually avoid a series of short sentences.

Beginnings

A long series of sentences with each beginning containing a subject followed by a verb may become monotonous. Consider beginning sentences in different ways:

> **With a prepositional phrase:** *In the distance* a dog barked.
> **With a transitional connective (conjunctive adverb) such as *then*, *however*, or *therefore*:** *Then* the game was over.
> **With a coordinating conjunction such as *and* or *but*:** *But* no one moved for three minutes.
> **With a dependent clause:** *Although Reggie wanted a new Corvette,* he settled for a used Ford Taurus.
> **With an adverb:** *Carefully* Sabrina removed the thorn from the lion's paw.

Exercise 6 Providing Sentence Variety

Revise the following passage to achieve better sentence variety through changes in types of sentences, order of information, length of sentences, and beginnings of sentences. Also, take care to avoid omission, and combine sentences for improved expression. Compare your revisions with those of others in your class. There is no single correct way of making these changes.

Power Rangers to the Rescue

Leewan Yeomans

I do promotions on the weekends for TV's "Power Rangers." I'm Trini. She's supposed to be Chinese. I'm Chinese American, the kids think I'm the real Ranger when I remove my mask. I've never felt very much like a Ranger except for one occasion. It was a weekend promotion, held at a park. We were doing our routine. I looked around and saw a little boy collapse. He had probably been in distress for a while. Wearing the mask, I could hardly see anything. Anyway, this little boy was lying there, thrashing around and trying to throw up. No one was doing anything. The Pink Ranger started running around trying to find the child's parents. I ran over when no one came to the aid of the boy, took off my mask, and put my finger in his mouth to clear his throat. There I found the problem. He had been chewing on, or maybe blowing, a long balloon. He had swallowed it. I pulled it out of his throat. It was almost a foot long. The whole spectacle must have looked like a magic trick. The child still wasn't breathing well. The paramedics were called. They quickly helped him back to good health. His parents, who lived across the street, came to carry him home. We Rangers put our masks back on. The audience cheered us as if we had planned the whole scene. We resumed our routine. It was just another day of work for the Power Rangers.

∼ Chapter Review

Exercise 7 Combining Sentences

Combine each pair of sentences into a single sentence by using any pattern.

1. Cobras are among the most feared of all snakes. They are not the deadliest of all snakes.

2. Cobras do not coil before they strike. They cannot strike over a long distance.

3. Cobras do not have a hood. They flatten their neck by moving their ribs when they are nervous or frightened.

4. Cobras inject venom with their fangs. They spit venom at their victims.

5. Human beings will not die from the venom that has been spit. It can cause blindness if it is not washed from the eyes.

6. A person can die from a cobra bite. Death may come in only a few hours.

7. Snake charmers have long worked with cobras. They use a snake, a basket, and a flute.

8. The snakes cannot *hear* the music. They respond to the rhythmic movements of the charmers.

9. The snake charmers are hardly ever in danger of being bitten. They defang the cobras or sew their mouths shut.

10. Most cobras will flee from people. They attack if they are cornered or if they are guarding their eggs.

Exercise 8   Combining Sentences

Combine each pair or group of sentences into a single sentence by using any pattern.

1. The original series, *Star Trek*, aired for only three years. Its first run was from 1966 to 1969.

2. The creator of the show was Gene Roddenberry. He had experience writing other television shows, especially Westerns.

3. *Star Trek* had low ratings. It had high production costs, as well.

4. It was canceled after just 79 episodes. The show has a huge cult following and is known throughout the world.

5. *Star Trek* became an enormously popular franchise. It gave rise to five television series as well as movies, games, and books.

6. The show involves the exploits of the starship *USS Enterprise*. Its crew explores the Milky Way galaxy.

7. Captain Kirk, First Officer Spock, Doctor McCoy, Lt. Uhura, and Lt. Commander Scott are some of the key characters. Others include Lt. Sulu and Ensign Chekov.

8. The show was groundbreaking. It featured elaborate set designs, intellectual themes, and a truly multicultural cast. Nichelle Nichols, as Lt. Uhura, was the first African-American woman to be cast in an important ongoing role in a television series.

9. First Officer Spock is extremely rational whereas Dr. McCoy is passionate. Captain Kirk is a combination of the two.

10. The show is loved by millions. It has spawned fan clubs and a huge memorabilia industry.

Exercise 9 Combining Sentences

Use appropriate methods to combine sentences as needed. Add and delete words sparingly.

Muhammad Ali was arguably the greatest heavyweight boxing champion. He won the title on four occasions. He loved to perform for the press. He made up sayings and poems about himself and his opponents. He once said he would "float like a butterfly and sting like a bee." Ali announced that he would win each fight. He even named the round. He became a Black Muslim. He refused induction into the armed services. He was convicted of a crime for having done so. As a result he lost his championship. Later the decision was reversed by the U.S. Supreme Court. He won back the championship by defeating George Foreman in 1974. In 1978 he lost it to Leon Spinks. He regained it the next year. He retired in 1980. He soon returned to the ring once more to fight for the championship. He quit for good.

5

Correcting Fragments, Comma Splices, and Run-Ons

In Chapters 1 and 2, you learned about parts of speech and subjects and verbs. In Chapters 3 and 4, you identified and wrote different kinds of sentences. With the information you now have, you will be able to spot and correct three problems that sometimes creep into what is otherwise good writing. Those problems are sentence fragments, comma splices, and run-on sentences.

⌒ Fragments

A correct sentence signals completeness. The structure and punctuation provide those signals. For example, if I say to you, "She left in a hurry," you do not necessarily expect me to say anything else, but if I say, "In a hurry," you do. If I say, "Tomorrow I will give you a quiz on the reading assignment," and I leave the room, you will merely take note of my words. But if I say, "Tomorrow when I give you a quiz on the reading assignment," and leave the room, you will probably be annoyed, and you may even chase after me and ask me to finish my sentence. Those examples illustrate the difference between completeness and incompleteness.

A **fragment** is a word or group of words without a subject ("Is going to town."), without a verb ("He going to town."), or without both ("Going to town."). A fragment can also be a group of words with a subject and verb that cannot stand alone ("When he goes to town."). Although the punctuation signals a sentence (a capital letter at the beginning and a period at the end), the structure of a fragment signals incompleteness. If you were to say or write a fragment to someone, that person would expect you to go on and finish the idea.

58

Other specific examples of common unacceptable fragments are the following:

- *Dependent clause only*: When she came.
- *Phrase(s) only*: Waiting there for some help.
- *No subject in main clause*: Went to the library.
- *No verb in main clause*: She being the only person there.

Dependent Clauses as Fragments: Clauses with Subordinating Conjunctions

In Chapter 3, you learned that words such as *because, after, although, since,* and *before* (see page 28 for a more complete list) are subordinating conjunctions, words that show the relationship of a dependent clause to an independent one. A dependent clause punctuated like a sentence (capital letter at the beginning; period at the end) is a sentence fragment.

While the ship was sinking.

You can choose one of many ways to fix that kind of fragment.

INCORRECT	They continued to dance. *While the ship was sinking.*
CORRECT	They continued to dance *while the ship was sinking.*
CORRECT	*While the ship was sinking,* they continued to dance.
CORRECT	The ship was sinking. They continued to dance.
CORRECT	The ship was sinking; they continued to dance.

In the first two correct sentences above, the dependent clause *while the ship was sinking* has been attached to an independent clause. In the next two sentences, the subordinating conjunction *while* has been omitted. The two independent clauses can then stand alone as sentences or as parts of a sentence, joined by a semicolon.

Dependent Clauses as Fragments: Clauses with Relative Pronouns

You also learned in Chapter 3 that words such as *that, which,* and *who* can function as relative pronouns, words that relate a clause back to a noun or pronoun in the sentence. Relative clauses are dependent. If they are punctuated as sentences (begin with a capital letter; end with a period), they are incorrect. They are really sentence fragments.

Which is lying on the floor.

The best way to fix such a fragment is to attach it as close as possible to the noun to which it refers.

INCORRECT   That new red sweater is mine. *Which is lying on the floor.*

CORRECT   The new red sweater, *which is lying on the floor*, is mine.

Reminder: Some relative clauses are restrictive (necessary to the meaning of the sentence) and should not be set off with commas. Some are nonrestrictive (not necessary to the meaning of the sentence), as in the example above, and are set off by commas.

Phrases as Fragments

Although a phrase may carry an idea, a phrase is a fragment because it is incomplete in structure. It lacks both a subject and a verb. In Chapter 2 we looked at verbal phrases and prepositional phrases, and in Chapter 4 we briefly discussed appositive phrases.

Verbal Phrase

INCORRECT   *Having studied hard all evening.* John decided to retire.

CORRECT   *Having studied hard all evening,* John decided to retire.

The italicized part of this example is a verbal phrase. As you learned in Chapter 2, a verbal is verblike without being a verb in sentence structure. Verbals include verb parts of speech ending in *-ed* and *-ing*. To correct a verbal phrase fragment, attach it to a complete sentence (an independent clause). When the phrase begins the sentence, it is usually set off by a comma.

Prepositional Phrase

INCORRECT   *After the last snow.* The workers built the road.

CORRECT   *After the last snow,* the workers built the road.

In this example, the fragment is a prepositional phrase—a group of words beginning with a preposition, such as *in, on, of, at,* and *with,* that connects a noun or pronoun object to the rest of the sentence. To correct a prepositional phrase fragment, attach it to a complete sentence (an independent clause). If the prepositional phrase is long and begins the sentence, it is usually set off by a comma.

Appositive Phrase

INCORRECT	Kevin lived in the small town of Whitman. *A busy industrial center near Boston.* (nonessential)
CORRECT	Kevin lived in the small town of Whitman, *a busy industrial center near Boston.*
INCORRECT	Many readers admire the work of the nineteenth-century American poet. *Emily Dickinson.* (essential)
CORRECT	Many readers admire the work of the nineteenth-century American poet *Emily Dickinson.*

In these examples, the fragment is an appositive phrase—a group of words following a noun or pronoun and renaming it. To correct an appositive phrase fragment, connect it to a complete sentence (an independent clause). An appositive phrase fragment is set off by a comma or by commas only if it is not essential to the sentence.

Fragments as Word Groups Without Subjects or Without Verbs

INCORRECT	Jermain studied many long hours. *And received the highest grade in the class.* (without subject)
CORRECT	Jermain studied many long hours *and received the highest grade in the class.*
INCORRECT	*Few children living in that section of the country.* (without verb)
CORRECT	*Few children live in that section of the country.*

Each conventional sentence must have an independent clause, meaning a word or a group of words that contains a subject and a verb and that can stand alone. As you may recall from the discussion of subjects in Chapter 2, a command or direction sentence, such as "Think," has an understood subject of *you.*

Acceptable Fragments

Sometimes fragments are used intentionally. When we speak, we often use the following fragments:

- *Interjections*: Great! Hooray! Whoa! Right!
- *Exclamations*: What a day! How terrible! What a bother! Are you serious!

- *Greetings*: Hello. Good morning. Good night. Good evening.
- *Questions*: What for? Why not? Where to?
- *Informal conversation*: (What time is it?) Eight o'clock. Really.

In novels, plays, and short stories, fragments are often used in conversation among characters. However, unless you are writing fiction, you need to be able to identify fragments in your college assignments and turn those fragments into complete sentences.

Exercise 1   Identifying Fragments

Identify each of the following as a fragment (FRAG) or a complete sentence (OK).

_____   1. Asia, which developed much earlier than the West.

_____   2. More than five thousand years ago, Asia had an advanced civilization.

_____   3. People there who invented writing and created literature.

_____   4. Involved in the development of science, agriculture, and religion.

_____   5. The birthplace of the major religions of the world.

_____   6. The most common religion in Asia being Hinduism.

_____   7. The second most common religion is Islam.

_____   8. Asia is the most populous continent.

_____   9. With almost four billion people.

_____   10. Hong Kong and Bangladesh, which are among the most densely populated places in the world.

Exercise 2 Correcting Fragments

Underline and correct each fragment. Some items may be correct as is.

1. When Leroy Robert Paige was seven years old. He was carrying luggage at a railroad station in Mobile, Alabama.

2. He was a clever young fellow. Who invented a contraption for carrying four satchels (small suitcases) at one time.

3. After he did that. He became known as Satchel Paige.

4. His fame rests on his being arguably the best baseball pitcher. Who ever played the game.

5. Because of the so-called Jim Crow laws. He, as an African American, was not allowed to play in the Major Leagues. Until 1948 after the Major League color barrier was broken.

6. By that time he was already forty-two. Although he was in excellent condition.

7. He had pitched. Wherever he could, mainly touring around the country.

8. When he faced Major Leaguers in exhibition games. He almost always won.

9. Because people liked to see him pitch. He pitched almost every day. While he was on tour.

10. One year he won 104 games. During his career he pitched 55 no-hitters and won more than 2,000 games.

11. He pitched his last game in the majors at the age of fifty-nine.

12. In 1971, he was the first African-American player. Who was voted into the Baseball Hall of Fame in a special category for those. Who played in the old Negro Leagues.

Exercise 3   Correcting Fragments

Underline and correct each fragment.

1. Although Woody Guthrie had a hard life. His songs are filled with hope.

2. His autobiography, *Bound for Glory*, tells of this free-spirited man. Who saw boomtown oil fields dry up and crops wither in the dust bowl.

3. Many people knew him only as the author of "This Land Is Your Land." Which is often treated as a second national anthem.

4. Because he was honest and would say what he thought. He was often out of work.

5. Cisco Houston said, "Woody is a man. Who writes two or three ballads before breakfast every morning."

6. The hobo, the migrant worker, the merchant marine, the sign painter, the labor agitator, the musician in New York City with his hat on the sidewalk—Woody was a restless traveler. Whose life was as varied as his song bag.

7. Some of his best songs are about his experience during the days of the Great Depression. When he was an unofficial spokesperson for migrant workers in the West.

8. Arlo Guthrie, Woody's son, achieved his own fame. While he carried on the folk music tradition of his father.

9. Woody's song "Pretty Boy Floyd" was recorded by Bob Dylan. Who modeled his early style on that of Woody and once referred to himself as a "Woody Guthrie jukebox."

10. A simple farmer once said to a reporter, "I'll always remember Woody as the man. Who said, 'Some men will rob you with a six-gun and some with a fountain pen.'"

Exercise 4   Correcting Fragments

Correct the fragments in any way you wish. Many can be fixed by combining word groups in this list. Write your complete sentences in the space provided.

1. Asia having many ethnic groups.

2. Including the Chinese, the Indians, the Arabs, the Turks, and the Jews.

3. The Chinese have different groups.

4. Speaking many dialects.

5. Although they have different dialects.

6. There is a national language.

7. A language called Mandarin.

8. Cultural differences exist in Taiwan.

9. The main difference being between the Chinese from the mainland and the Taiwanese.

10. Despite the differences, all Chinese have much culture in common.

～ Comma Splices and Run-Ons

The comma splice and the run-on are two other kinds of faulty "sentences" that give false signals to the reader. In each instance, the punctuation suggests that there is only one sentence, but, in fact, there is material for two.

The **comma splice** consists of two independent clauses with only a comma between them:

> *The weather was disappointing,* <u>we canceled the picnic.</u> (A comma by itself cannot join two independent clauses.)

The **run-on** differs from the comma splice in only one respect: It has no comma between the independent clauses. Therefore, the run-on is two independent clauses with *nothing* between them:

> *The weather was disappointing* <u>we canceled the picnic.</u> (Independent clauses must be properly connected.)

Because an independent clause can stand by itself as a sentence and because two independent clauses must be properly linked, you can use a simple technique to identify the comma splice and the run-on. If you see a sentence that you think may contain one of these two errors, ask yourself this question: "Can I insert a period at some place in the word group and still have a sentence on either side?" If the answer is yes and there is no word such as *and* or *but* following the inserted period, then you have a comma splice or a run-on to correct. In our previous examples of the comma splice and the run-on, we could insert a period after the word *disappointing* in each case, and we would still have an independent clause—therefore, a sentence—on either side.

Correcting Comma Splices and Run-Ons

Once you identify a comma splice or a run-on in your writing, you need to correct it. Use one of these four different ways to fix these common sentence problems: use a comma and a coordinating conjunction, use a subordinating conjunction, use a semicolon, or make each clause a separate sentence.

Use a Comma and a Coordinating Conjunction

INCORRECT   We canceled the picnic the weather was disappointing. (run-on)

CORRECT   We canceled the picnic, *for* the weather was disappointing. (Here we inserted a comma and the coordinating conjunction *for*.)

Knowing the seven coordinating conjunctions will help you in writing sentences and correcting sentence problems. Remember the acronym FANBOYS: *for, and, nor, but, or, yet, so*.

Exercise 5 Correcting Comma Splices and Run-Ons

Identify each word group as a comma splice (CS), a run-on (RO), or a complete sentence (OK), and correct the errors using commas and coordinating conjunctions.

EXAMPLE: __CS__ He did the assignment, ^his boss gave him a bonus.
and

_____ 1. In 1846, a group of eighty-two settlers headed for California with much optimism, a hard road lay ahead.

_____ 2. They had expected to cross the mountains before winter they were in good spirits.

_____   3. They would not arrive in California before winter, nor would some of them get there at all.

_____   4. When they encountered a heavy snowstorm, they stopped to spend the winter they still thought they would be safe.

_____   5. They made crude shelters of logs and branches some also used moss and earth.

_____   6. They had trouble managing, they had not encountered such problems before.

_____   7. They ran out of regular food they ate roots, mice, shoe leather, and their horses.

_____   8. Thirty-five members of the Donner Party died that winter the survivors were so hungry that they ate the dead bodies.

_____   9. They were weak, sick, and depressed they did not give up.

_____   10. Fifteen people set out to get help seven survived and returned to rescue friends and relatives.

Exercise 6   Correcting Comma Splices and Run-Ons

Identify each word group as a comma splice (CS), a run-on (RO), or a complete sentence (OK), and correct the errors using commas and coordinating conjunctions.

_____   1. Comedian Woody Allen once observed that no one gets out of this world alive, we all know that no human is immortal.

_____   2. But several famous dead people have managed to continue to _look_ alive they (or their admirers) had their bodies preserved and put on display.

_____   3. Philosopher Jeremy Bentham wanted his body preserved, his wishes were carried out when he died in 1832.

———————— 4. Bentham left a lot of money to London's University College, the college couldn't have the money unless it agreed to let Bentham's body attend its annual board of directors meetings.

———————— 5. Bentham's dressed-up body was posed sitting in an armchair in his hand was his favorite walking stick.

———————— 6. Every year for ninety-two years, the college complied with Bentham's instructions the board's minutes for those years record Bentham as "present but not voting."

———————— 7. Bentham's body is still at University College, it's on display now in a permanent exhibit.

———————— 8. V. I. Lenin, leader of the former Soviet Union, has been dead and on display since 1924 Russians and tourists can still visit his lifelike body enclosed in a glass coffin in Moscow.

———————— 9. The corpse of People's Republic of China founder Mao Zedong was preserved for posterity, too, in his mausoleum, an elevator raises his glass coffin from underground to a public viewing area every morning.

———————— 10. Other famous people turned into modern mummies were national leaders Joseph Stalin, Eva Perón, and Ho Chi Minh, and opera singer Enrico Caruso.

Use a Subordinating Conjunction

INCORRECT   The weather was disappointing, we canceled the picnic.

CORRECT   *Because* the weather was disappointing, we canceled the picnic.

By inserting the subordinating conjunction *because*, you can transform the first independent clause into a dependent clause and correct the comma splice. Knowing common subordinating conjunctions will help you in writing sentences and correcting sentence problems. Here is a list of the subordinating conjunctions you saw in Chapters 3 and 4. Each of these words indicates a particular relationship between the ideas being connected.

after	if	until
although	in order that	when
as	provided that	whenever
as if	rather than	where
because	since	whereas
before	so that	wherever
even if	than	whether
even though	unless	while

Exercise 7   Correcting Comma Splices and Run-Ons

Identify each word group as a comma splice (CS), a run-on (RO), or a complete sentence (OK), and correct the errors by making a dependent clause.

_____   1. Jesse Owens won four gold medals in the 1936 Olympics he became a famous person.

_____   2. The 1936 Olympics were held in Nazi Germany Owens was placed at a disadvantage.

_____   3. Hitler believed in the superiority of the Aryans, he thought Owens would lose.

_____   4. Jesse Owens an African American won Hitler showed his disappointment openly.

_____   5. Owens broke a record for the 200-meter race that had stood for thirty-six years.

_____   6. Owens then jumped a foot farther than others in the long jump Hitler left the stadium.

_____   7. Before the day was at last over, Owens had also won gold medals in the 100-meter dash and the 400-meter relay.

_____   8. Hitler's early departure was a snub at Owens, but Jesse did not care.

_____ 9. Owens returned to the United States, he engaged in numerous exhibitions, including racing against a horse.

_____ 10. In his later years Owens became an official for the U.S. Olympic Committee, he never received the recognition that many contemporary athletes do.

Exercise 8 Correcting Comma Splices and Run-Ons

Identify each word group as a comma splice (CS), a run-on (RO), or a complete sentence (OK), and correct the errors by making a dependent clause.

_____ 1. Roberto Clemente grew up poor in Puerto Rico, he would become rich and famous.

_____ 2. As a child he was determined to play baseball he used a tree limb to slug an old tennis ball wrapped with yarn.

_____ 3. Clemente excelled in youth and sandlot teams, he signed a contract to play professional baseball.

_____ 4. He played for the Pittsburgh Pirates between 1955 and 1972, he was once selected the Most Valuable Player and twice had the highest hitting average in the National League.

_____ 5. Often regarded as the best right fielder of all time, he won twelve Gold Gloves for his defensive play, and it was said he could throw out runners from his knees.

_____ 6. Clemente said that he was taught good values by his family and that he respected the poor because they had learned about life from their suffering.

_____ 7. Clemente became wealthy, he always found time to help the less fortunate.

_____   8. He liked to take an active part in his humanitarian work, in 1972 he decided to fly on an airplane he had chartered to take supplies to earthquake victims in Nicaragua.

_____   9. The airplane crashed all aboard were killed.

_____   10. He was a great baseball player and a great human being many schools and parks have been named after him.

Use a Semicolon

INCORRECT   The weather was disappointing, we canceled the picnic.

CORRECT   The weather was disappointing; we canceled the picnic.

CORRECT   The weather was disappointing; *therefore,* we canceled the picnic.

This comma splice was corrected by a semicolon. The first correct example shows the semicolon alone. The second correct example shows a semicolon followed by the conjunctive adverb *therefore* and a comma. The conjunctive adverb is optional, but, as we have already seen, conjunctive adverbs can make the relationship between independent clauses stronger. Here is the list of conjunctive adverbs you saw in Chapter 4.

however	on the other hand
otherwise	then
therefore	consequently
similarly	also
hence	thus

Recall the acronym HOTSHOT CAT, made up of the first letter of each of these common conjunctive adverbs. The acronym will help you remember them. Other conjunctive adverbs include *in fact, for example, moreover, nevertheless, furthermore, now, on the one hand,* and *soon.*

 Exercise 9   Correcting Comma Splices and Run-Ons

Identify each word group as a comma splice (CS), a run-on (RO), or a complete sentence (OK). Make corrections with a semicolon, and add a conjunctive adverb if appropriate.

_____ 1. Harry Houdini is often referred to as a magician, he was more famous as an escapologist.

_____ 2. He initially performed card tricks and other common routines of illusion, he developed some special nonescape acts.

_____ 3. One of his spectacular nonescape acts was making an elephant and its trainer disappear they were actually lowered into an empty swimming pool under the stage.

_____ 4. Soon Houdini grew bored with conventional magic, and he perfected some escape tricks.

_____ 5. Houdini learned to swallow and then regurgitate keys and tools, he could break free from restraints under water.

_____ 6. Houdini could also dislocate both shoulders at will he could escape easily from a straitjacket.

_____ 7. Houdini's most famous trick involved the Chinese Water Torture Cell, a steel and glass water-filled box in which he was chained and suspended upside down.

_____ 8. As an active member of a group of skeptics, he exposed spiritualists who claimed to contact the dead.

_____ 9. He decided to put his beliefs to a test, shortly before his death, he gave his wife a secret code and told her he would try to contact her from the grave.

_____ 10. Each Halloween night for a decade after he died, his wife and friends met and waited for a signal from Houdini, she gave up, saying, "Ten years is long enough to wait for any man."

Make Each Clause a Separate Sentence

INCORRECT   The weather was disappointing, we canceled the picnic.

CORRECT   The weather was disappointing. We canceled the picnic.

To correct the comma splice, replace the comma with a period, and begin the second sentence (the second independent clause) with a capital letter. This method is at once the simplest and most common method of correcting comma splices and run-ons. For a run-on, insert a period between the two independent clauses and begin the second sentence with a capital letter.

Exercise 10   Correcting Comma Splices and Run-Ons

Identify each word group as a comma splice (CS), a run-on (RO), or a complete sentence (OK). Correct the errors with a period and a capital letter.

_____   1. The world's fastest steel track roller coaster is the Top Thrill Dragster it's at the Cedar Point Amusement Park in Ohio.

_____   2. Riders rocket out of a starting gate they reach a speed of 120 miles per hour in four seconds.

_____   3. The second-fastest roller coaster is in Japan it goes a mere 106.8 miles per hour.

_____   4. Wooden roller coasters are downright pokey in comparison the fastest reaches speeds of only 78.3 miles per hour.

_____   5. If you're looking for the biggest drop, the Top Thrill Dragster has that distinction, too.

_____   6. The largest drop on the Top Thrill Dragster is 400 feet, compare that to the largest drop on a wooden coaster, which is only 214 feet.

_____   7. The longest roller coaster ride of them all is the Steel Dragon 2000 in Japan that coaster is 8,133 feet long.

_____   8. You want the steepest angle of descent you can choose from several steel track coasters that allow you to plummet downward at a 90-degree angle.

_____   9. The steepest wooden coasters average about 55 degrees as a matter of fact, the steepest of all is only 61 degrees.

_____   10. These world's record-setting roller coasters have provided much excitement to million's of people, and thrill-seekers hope they'll continue to get faster and steeper.

⌒ Chapter Review

Exercise 11 Correcting Fragments, Comma Splices, and Run-Ons

Identify each word group as a comma splice (CS), a run-on (RO), a fragment (FRAG), or a complete sentence (OK). Correct the faulty sentences.

_____   1. Piranhas live in freshwater streams and rivers of South America, they travel through the water in groups.

_____   2. These ferocious-looking fish have a protruding lower jaw revealing a mouthful of sharp teeth.

_____   3. Piranhas are meat-eaters they will eat just about any live or dead creature.

_____   4. A school of piranhas consuming an animal the size of a pig in just minutes.

_____   5. Like sharks, they are drawn toward the scent of blood in the water, movements such as splashing attract them, too.

_____   6. When a school of piranhas is in a feeding frenzy.

_____   7. The water appears to boil and become red with blood.

_____   8. The piranha owes its savage reputation, in part, to adventurer Theodore Roosevelt.

_____   9. Who wrote in a 1914 book that these ruthless predators would "devour alive any man or beast."

_____   10. Roosevelt had heard of a man who went out alone on a mule, the mule returned to camp without its rider.

_____   11. The man's skeleton was found in the water every bit of flesh had been stripped from his bones.

_____   12. Still, Americans intrigued by stories bought piranhas for aquarium pets.

_____   13. Fascinated by the fish's grisly reputation.

_____   14. Perhaps admiring the silver body and bright red belly of this handsome creature.

_____   15. As aquarium owners realized that their pets could be quite aggressive and dangerous.

_____   16. Piranhas dumped into ponds, lakes, and reservoirs across the United States.

_____   17. Fortunately, most of the waters were too cold for the piranhas to survive.

_____   18. Truthfully, though, piranhas rarely attack humans, South Americans even bathe in piranha-infested waters.

_____   19. South Americans also think piranhas are tasty and like to net, cook, and eat them.

_____   20. However, U.S. officials are taking no chances, piranhas are illegal in many states.

Exercise 12 Correcting Fragments, Comma Splices, and Run-Ons

Correct each fragment, comma splice, and run-on. Choose which-ever method of correction works best for each sentence problem.

Deserts are often referred to as wastelands. It is true that not as many plants grow there as grow in temperate zones, it is also true that animals do not live there in great numbers. But many plants and animals live and do quite well in the desert. Because of their adaptations.

Not all deserts have the same appearance. Many people think of the desert as a hot, sandy area. Actually sand covers only about 20 percent of the desert. Some deserts have mountains some others have snow.

Because deserts are dry for most of the year. Plants must conserve and store water. Several kinds of cacti can shrink during a dry season and swell during a rainy season. Some shrubs simply drop their leaves and use their green bark to manufacture chlorophyll. Seeds sometimes lying in the desert for several years before sprouting to take advantage of a rainfall.

Animals have quite effectively adjusted to the desert, some animals obtain moisture from the food they eat and require no water. One animal of the desert, the camel, produces fat. Which it stores in its hump. The fat allows the camel to reserve more body heat it needs little water. Still other animals feed only at night or are inactive for weeks or even months.

About 15 percent of the land of the earth is covered by deserts. That area increasing every year. Because of overgrazing by livestock. Also because of the destruction of forests. Areas that were once green and fertile will now support little life and only a small population of human beings.

6

Balancing Sentence Parts

We are surrounded by balance. Watch a colorful cross-frame, or diamond, kite as it soars in the sky. If you draw an imaginary line from the top to the bottom of the kite, you will see corresponding parts on either side. If you were to replace one of the sides with a loose-flapping fabric, the kite would never fly. A similar lack of balance can also cause a sentence to crash.

Consider these statements:

> "*To be* or not *to be*—that is the question." (dash added)

This line from *Hamlet*, by William Shakespeare, is one of the most famous in literature. Compare it to the well-balanced kite in a strong wind. Its parts are parallel and it "flies" well.

> "*To be* or *not being*—that is the question."

This line still vaguely resembles the sleek kite, but now the altered phrase causes it to dip like an unbalanced kite. Lurching, the line begins to lose altitude.

> "*To be* or *death is the other alternative*—that is the question."

With that change in wording, the line loses its balance and slams to the floor. Words scatter across the carpet. We must glance back at the original version and admit that Shakespeare had it right in the beginning.

The first sentence is forceful and easy to read. The second is more difficult to follow. The third is almost impossible to understand. We understand it only because we know what it should look like from having read the original. The point is that perceptive readers are as critical of sentences as kite-watchers are of kites.

∿ Basic Principles of Parallelism

Parallelism as it relates to sentence structure is usually achieved by joining words with similar words: nouns with nouns, adjectives

78

(words that can describe nouns) with adjectives, adverbs (words that can describe verbs) with adverbs, and so forth.

> *Men*, *women*, and *children* enjoy the show. (nouns)
>
> The players are *excited*, *eager*, and *enthusiastic*. (adjectives)
>
> The author wrote *skillfully* and *quickly*. (adverbs)

Parallel structure may also be achieved by joining groups of words with other similar groups of words: prepositional phrase with prepositional phrase, clause with clause, sentence with sentence.

> She fell *in love* and *out of love* in a few minutes. (prepositional phrases)
>
> *Who he was* and *where he came from* did not matter. (clauses)
>
> *He came in a hurry. He left in a hurry.* (sentences)

Parallelism means balancing one structure with another of the same kind. Faulty parallel structure is awkward and draws unfavorable attention to what is being said.

> NONPARALLEL   LeBron James's reputation is based on his ability in *passing, shooting,* and *he is good at rebounds.*
>
> PARALLEL   LeBron James's reputation is based on his ability in *passing, shooting,* and *rebounding.*

In the first example, the words *passing* and *shooting* are of the same kind (verblike words used as nouns), but the rest of the sentence is different. You don't have to know terms to realize that there is a problem in smoothness and emphasis. Just read the material aloud. Then compare it with the parallel statement; *he is good at rebounds* is changed to *rebounding* to make a sentence that's easy on the eye and ear.

⌒ Signal Words

Some words signal parallel structure. If you use *and*, the items joined by *and* should almost always be parallel. If they aren't, then *and* is probably inappropriate.

> The weather is hot *and* humid. (*and* joins adjectives)
>
> The car *and* the trailer are parked in front of the house. (*and* joins nouns)

The same principle is true for *but*, although it implies a direct contrast. Where contrasts are being drawn, parallel structure is essential to clarify those contrasts.

> Ming *purchased* a Dodger Dog, *but* I *chose* the Stadium Peanuts. (*but* joins contrasting clauses)

> Kachina *made* an A in math *but* *failed* her art class. (*but* joins contrasting verbs)

You should regard all the coordinating conjunctions (FANBOYS) as signals for parallel structure.

Exercise 1   Identifying Signal Words and Parallel Elements

Underline the parallel elements—words, phrases, or clauses—and circle the signal words in the following sentences. The words and phrases within parentheses are movie titles.

1. During the Vietnam War, an army colonel named Kurtz has gone mad, so an army captain is sent on a top-secret mission to investigate and assassinate him. (*Apocalypse Now*)

2. The new kid, Jim, is forced to take part in a deadly game of "chicken" with a bully and gang leader, Buzz. (*Rebel Without a Cause*)

3. In the Brazilian Amazon, a fossil of a web-footed creature is found, and the search for more fossils begins. (*Creature from the Black Lagoon*)

4. Two New York slum kids, Rocky and Jerry, are caught stealing, but only Rocky is apprehended. (*Angels with Dirty Faces*)

5. Fourteen-year-old Mattie Ross wants vengeance on her father's killer, so she hires a one-eyed U.S. marshall to do the job. (*True Grit*)

6. Blanche DuBois and Stella Kowalski are sisters with very different life paths. (*A Streetcar Named Desire*)

7. Stella has chosen to live a simple life with a "common man," but Blanche has lived in a romantic world of denial. (*A Streetcar Named Desire*)

8. A man flees a disturbed past while being pursued by a lawman, a psychopathic killer, and the woman who still loves him. (*Night Breed*)

9. A man wants money he didn't earn, a sightless woman wants to see, and another man wants to escape from his past. (*Night Gallery*)

10. Norman Bates attempts to put his life together and to put his old habits behind him. (*Psycho III*)

⁓ Combination Signal Words

The words *and* and *but* are the most common individual signal words used with parallel constructions. Sometimes, however, **combination words** signal the need for parallelism or balance. The most common ones are *either/or*, *neither/nor*, *not only/but also*, *both/and*, and *whether/or*. Now consider the following faulty sentences and two types of corrections:

NONPARALLEL *Either* we will win this game, *or* let's go out fighting.

PARALLEL *Either we will* win this game, *or we will* go out fighting.

The correction is made by changing *let's* to *we will* to parallel the *we will* in the first part of the sentence. The same construction should follow the *either* and the *or*.

NONPARALLEL   Flour is used *not only* to bake cakes *but also* in
                paste.

PARALLEL   Flour is used *not only to bake* cakes *but also to
                make* paste.

The correction is made by changing *in* (a preposition) to *to make*
(an infinitive). Now an infinitive follows both *not only* and *but also*.

Exercise 2 Identifying Combination Signal Words
                and Parallel Elements

*Underline the parallel elements—words, phrases, or clauses—and
circle the combination signal words in the following sentences.*

1. Robin Hood not only robbed from the rich but also gave to the

   poor. (*Adventures of Robin Hood*, 1938)

2. Both Humphrey Bogart and Katharine Hepburn star in this

   movie about two unlikely people traveling together through

   the jungle rivers of Africa during World War I. (*The African

   Queen*)

3. Dr. Jekyll discovers a potion, and now he can be either himself

   or Mr. Hyde. (*Dr. Jekyll and Mr. Hyde*)

4. An Oklahoma family moves to California and finds neither

   good jobs nor compassion in the "promised land." (*The Grapes

   of Wrath*)

5. In this Christmas classic, Jimmy Stewart stars as a man who

   can either die by suicide or go back to see what life would have

   been like without him. (*It's a Wonderful Life*)

6. During the Korean War, army surgeons discover that they must either develop a lunatic lifestyle or go crazy. (*M*A*S*H*)

7. An advertising executive not only gets tied up with an obnoxious and boring salesman but also goes with him on a wacky chase across the country. (*Planes, Trains, and Automobiles*)

8. In this flawless integration of animation and live action, Roger and Eddie try to discover both who framed Roger and who is playing patty-cake with his wife. (*Who Framed Roger Rabbit?*)

9. A long-suffering black woman named Celie experiences not only heartaches but also some joy as she rises from tragedy to personal triumph. (*The Color Purple*)

10. An independent man learns that he is expected to give up either his dignity or his life. (*Cool Hand Luke*)

⌒ Chapter Review

Exercise 3 Completing Sentences with Parallel Elements

Complete each of the following sentences by adding a word, phrase, or clause that is parallel to the italicized word, phrase, or clause.

1. We went to the zoo not only for *fun* but also for _____

   _____

2. He attended Utah State University for *a good education* and __

   _____

3. For a college major, she was considering *English, history,* and __

   _____

4. Mr. Ramos was a *good neighbor* and _____

   _____

5. My diet for breakfast that week consisted of *a slice of bread, a glass of low-fat milk*, and _____

   _____

6. She decided that she must choose between *a social life* and ____

   _____

7. Either *she would make the choice*, or _____

   _____

8. Because we are mutually supportive, either *we will all have a good time*, or _____

   _____

9. Like the Three Musketeers, our motto is *"All for one*, and ____

   _____

10. My intention was to *work a year, save my money*, and _____

   _____

Exercise 4   Writing Sentences with Parallel Elements

Use each of the following signal words or combination signal words in a sentence of eight or more words about the topic food.

1. and _____

   _____

2. but _____

   _____

3. so _____

   _____

4. either/or _____

   _____

5. both/and _____

   _____

7

Verbs

For good reasons, verbs claim the most chapter pages in this book. As keystone words, verbs indicate the action, being, or state of being of the subject. Verbs focus on the idea(s) you want to deliver to your audience, and in the most effective communication; they do so by using the kinds of words your audience expects. *Audience* pertains to your reason for communicating, the situation, and the persons(s) who will receive your message. This chapter will apply to some of your major concerns for college writing, workplace messages, and personal communication: verb tenses for regular and irregular verbs, subject-verb agreement, consistency in tense, active and passive voice, and strong verbs.

~ Regular and Irregular Verbs

Verbs can be divided into two categories, called *regular* and *irregular*. Regular verbs are predictable, but irregular verbs—as the term suggests—follow no definite pattern.

Verbs always show time. Present-tense verbs show an action or a state of being that is occurring at the present time: I *like* your hat. Mike *is* at a hockey game right now. Present-tense verbs can also imply a continuation from the past into the future: Carmen *drives* to work every day.

Past-tense verbs show an action or a state of being that occurred in the past: We *walked* to town yesterday. Bao *was* president of the club last year.

Regular Verbs

Present Tense

For *he, she,* and *it,* regular verbs in the present tense add an -*s* or an -*es* to the base word. The following chart shows the present tense of the base word *ask,* which is a regular verb.

	Singular	**Plural**
FIRST PERSON	I ask	we ask
SECOND PERSON	you ask	you ask
THIRD PERSON	he, she, it asks	they ask

If the verb ends in -*y*, you might have to drop the -*y* and add -*ies* for *he, she,* and *it.*

	Singular	**Plural**
FIRST PERSON	I try	we try
SECOND PERSON	you try	you try
THIRD PERSON	he, she, it tries	they try

Past Tense

For regular verbs in the past tense, add -*ed* to the base form:

Base Form (Present)	**Past**
walk	walked
answer	answered

If the base form already ends in -*e*, add just -*d*:

Base Form (Present)	**Past**
smile	smiled
decide	decided

If the base form ends in a consonant followed by -*y*, drop the -*y* and add -*ied*.

Base Form (Present)	**Past**
fry	fried
amplify	amplified

Regardless of how you form the past tense, regular verbs in the past tense do not change forms. The following chart shows the past tense of the base word *like,* which is a regular verb.

	Singular	**Plural**
FIRST PERSON	I liked	we liked
SECOND PERSON	you liked	you liked
THIRD PERSON	he, she, it liked	they liked

Past Participles

The past participle uses the helping verbs *has, have,* or *had* along with the past tense of the verb. For regular verbs, the past participle form of the verb is the same as the past tense.

Base Form	Past	Past Participle
happen	happened	happened
hope	hoped	hoped
cry	cried	cried

Following is a list of some common regular verbs, showing the base form, the past tense, and the past participle. The base form can also be used with such helping verbs as *can, could, do, does, did, may, might, must, shall, should, will,* and *would.*

Regular Verbs

Base Form (Present)	Past	Past Participle
ask	asked	asked
answer	answered	answered
cry	cried	cried
decide	decided	decided
dive	dived (dove)	dived
drag	dragged	dragged
finish	finished	finished
happen	happened	happened
learn	learned	learned
like	liked	liked
love	loved	loved
need	needed	needed
open	opened	opened
start	started	started
suppose	supposed	supposed
walk	walked	walked
want	wanted	wanted

Irregular Verbs

Irregular verbs do not follow any definite pattern.

Base Form (Present)	Past	Past Participle
shake	shook	shaken

make	made	made
begin	began	begun

Some irregular verbs that sound similar in the present tense don't follow the same pattern.

Base Form (Present)	Past	Past Participle
ring	rang	rung
swing	swung	swung
bring	brought	brought

Present Tense

For *he, she,* and *it,* irregular verbs in the present tense add an *-s* or an *-es* to the base word. The following chart shows the present tense of the base word *break,* which is an irregular verb.

	Singular	Plural
FIRST PERSON	I break	we break
SECOND PERSON	you break	you break
THIRD PERSON	he, she, it breaks	they break

If the irregular verb ends in *-y,* you might have to drop the *-y* and add *-ies* for *he, she,* and *it.*

	Singular	Plural
FIRST PERSON	I fly	we fly
SECOND PERSON	you fly	you fly
THIRD PERSON	he, she, it flies	they fly

Past Tense

Like past-tense regular verbs, past-tense irregular verbs do not change their forms. The following chart shows the past tense of the irregular verb *do.*

	Singular	Plural
FIRST PERSON	I did	we did
SECOND PERSON	you did	you did
THIRD PERSON	he, she, it did	they did

Past Participles

Following is a list of some common irregular verbs, showing the base form (present), the past tense, and the past participle. Like regular verbs, the base forms can be used with such helping verbs as *can, could, do, does, did, may, might, must, shall, should, will,* and *would*.

Irregular Verbs

Base Form (Present)	Past	Past Participle
arise	arose	arisen
awake	awoke (awaked)	awaked
be	was, were	been
become	became	become
begin	began	begun
bend	bent	bent
blow	blew	blown
break	broke	broken
bring	brought	brought
buy	bought	bought
catch	caught	caught
choose	chose	chosen
cling	clung	clung
come	came	come
creep	crept	crept
deal	dealt	dealt
do	did	done
drink	drank	drunk
drive	drove	driven
eat	ate	eaten
feel	felt	felt
fight	fought	fought
fling	flung	flung
fly	flew	flown
forget	forgot	forgotten
freeze	froze	frozen
get	got	got (gotten)
go	went	gone
grow	grew	grown
have	had	had
know	knew	known

(continued)

Base Form (Present)	Past	Past Participle
lead	led	led
leave	left	left
lose	lost	lost
mean	meant	meant
read	read	read
ride	rode	ridden
ring	rang	rung
see	saw	seen
shine	shone	shone
shine	shined	shined
shoot	shot	shot
sing	sang	sung
sink	sank	sunk
sleep	slept	slept
slink	slunk	slunk
speak	spoke	spoken
spend	spent	spent
steal	stole	stolen
stink	stank (stunk)	stunk
sweep	swept	swept
swim	swam	swum
swing	swung	swung
take	took	taken
teach	taught	taught
tear	tore	torn
think	thought	thought
throw	threw	thrown
wake	woke (waked)	woken (waked)
weep	wept	wept
write	wrote	written

～ "Problem" Verbs

The following pairs of verbs are especially troublesome and confusing: *lie* and *lay*, *sit* and *set*, and *rise* and *raise*. One way to tell them apart is to remember which word in each pair takes a direct object. A direct object answers the question *whom* or *what* in connection with a verb. The words *lay*, *raise*, and *set* take a direct object.

He *raised* the window. (He *raised* what?)

Lie, rise, and *sit,* however, cannot take a direct object. We cannot say, for example, "He rose the window." In the following examples, the italicized words are objects.

Present Tense	Meaning	Past Tense	Past Participle	Example
lie	to rest	lay	lain	I lay down to rest.
lay	to place something	laid	laid	We laid the *books* on the table.
rise	to go up	rose	risen	The smoke rose quickly.
raise	to lift	raised	raised	She raised the *question.*
sit	to rest	sat	sat	He sat in the chair.
set	to place something	set	set	They set the *basket* on the floor.

∿ The Twelve Verb Tenses at a Glance

Some languages, such as Chinese and Navajo, have no verb tenses to indicate time. English has a fairly complicated system of tenses, but most verbs pattern in what are known as the simple tenses: past, present, and future. Altogether there are twelve tenses in English. The following charts present those tenses in sentences, explain what the different tenses mean, and show how to form them.

Simple Tenses

PRESENT (may imply a continuation from past to future)	I, we, you, they *drive.* He, she, it *drives.*
PAST	I, we, you, he, she, it, they *drove.*
FUTURE	I, we, you, he, she, it, they *will drive.*

Perfect Tenses

PRESENT PERFECT (completed recently in the past; may continue into the present)	I, we, you, they *have driven.* He, she, it *has driven.*
PAST PERFECT (completed prior to a specific time in the past)	I, we, you, he, she, it, they *had driven.*
FUTURE PERFECT (will occur at a time prior to a specific time in the future)	I, we, you, he, she, it, they *will have driven.*

Progressive Tenses

PRESENT PROGRESSIVE (in progress now)	I *am driving.* He, she, it *is driving.* You, they *are driving.*
PAST PROGRESSIVE (in progress in the past)	I, he, she, it *was driving.* You, they *were driving.*
FUTURE PROGRESSIVE (in progress in the future)	I, you, he, she, it, they *will be driving.*

Perfect Progressive Tenses

PRESENT PERFECT PROGRESSIVE (in progress up to now)	I, you, they *have been driving.* He, she, it *has been driving.*
PAST PERFECT PROGRESSIVE (in progress before another event in the past)	I, you, he, she, it, they *had been driving.*
FUTURE PERFECT PROGRESSIVE (in progress before another event in the future)	I, you, he, she, it, they *will have been driving.*

Exercise 1   Selecting (Troublesome) Verbs

Underline the correct verb form.

1. According to legend, a vampire (lays, lies) in his coffin during the daylight hours.

2. Like a teenager, he (sets, sits) his own schedule: he sleeps all day and stays out all night.

3. He cannot (rise, raise) until after the sun sets.

4. Then the bloodsucker can (rise, raise) the coffin's lid and (set, sit) up.

5. He (rises, raises) from his bed hungry.

6. But don't bother (setting, sitting) a place for him at the dinner table.

7. He goes out hunting for victims who have unwisely (lain, laid) down their crucifixes, wooden stakes, and garlic necklaces.

8. He pounces quickly so that the victim has no time to (rise, raise) an alarm.

9. If he (lies, lays) his hands upon you, you're a "goner."

10. But when the sun begins to (rise, raise) in the sky, this monster must hurry back to bed to (lie, lay) his head down.

11. The book is (laying, lying) on top of the TV set.

12. When the manager came into the room, he (raised, rose) and saluted.

13. With his eyes closed, my dad can (sit, set) in his easy chair and watch TV for hours.

14. Why are you (setting, sitting) my orchids in the hot sun?

15. It's time to (lie, lay) down and nap for a few hours.

16. The cost of a good hamburger has (raised, risen) during the hoof and mouth epidemic.

17. It's time to (lay, lie) the issue aside and eat our fine meal.

18. She (rose, raised) the window and waved to me prettily.

19. When Joey proposed marriage, Ruth (raised, rose) an important question about his unemployment issue.

20. He smacked his lips noisily and (lay, laid) a dime tip on the counter.

Exercise 2   Selecting Verbs

Underline the correct verb form.

1. I wished I (stayed, had stayed) home.

2. I remembered that I (paid, had paid) him twice.

3. After parking their car, they (walk, walked) to the beach.

4. I (have, had) never encountered a genius until I met her.

5. I hoped that we (could have gone, went) to the big game.

6. They know that they (will complete, will have completed) the job before the first snow.

7. We (are considering, consider) the proposal.

8. He told us of the interesting life he (had led, led).

9. We went to the desert to see the cabin they (built, had built).

10. Tomorrow I (drive, will drive) to the supermarket for party items.

Exercise 3 Selecting Verbs

Underline the correct verb form.

1. The scholars (worked, had worked) many hours before they
   solved the problem.

2. The shipping clerks wished they (had sent, sent) the package.

3. We (study, are studying) the issue now.

4. We (decide, will decide) on the winner tomorrow.

5. They reminded us that we (made, had made) the same promise
   before.

6. Before Teena went to Mexico, she (had never been, never was)
   out of the country.

7. Jake (had been napping, napped) when the alarm sounded.

8. By the time he finished talking, he realized that he (said, had
   said) too much.

9. At the end of the semester, the course grade (depends, will
   depend) on your ability to write well.

10. After he retired, I realized how much I (had learned, learned)
    from working with him.

Exercise 4 Selecting Verbs

Underline the correct verb form.

1. Foods similar to pizza (have, had) been around for a long time.

2. Flat breads like focaccia are (knowed, known) to have been around for thousands of years in the Mediterranean region.

3. Naples in the 1500s (begun, began) to have a type of peasant food called *pizza*.

4. The tomato sauce, cheese, and other familiar toppings (appears, appeared) later, in the 1700s around Naples.

5. Italian aficionados of pizza only (recognize, recognized) two types of "real" pizza: the Margherita and the Marinara.

6. Both types start with hand-kneaded dough that is (lain, laid) in a wood-fired, and domed oven.

7. Neither (have, has) many toppings, but they feature tomato sauce.

8. Italian immigrants first (bring, brought) pizza to the United States around the turn of the twentieth century to cities like New York and Boston, but it remained mainly in the immigrant communities.

9. U.S. soldiers discovered the delicious food in Europe during World War II and (began, begin) opening pizza restaurants when they got back home.

10. Pizza's popularity (sweeps, swept) through the nation, and now there are tens of thousands of pizza restaurants in the United

States, though mostly chains rather than the "mom and pop" establishments of the 1950s.

Exercise 5 Choosing Verb Tense

Underline the correct verb form.

1. We (study, are studying) William Shakespeare's play *Romeo and Juliet*.

2. The teenagers Romeo and Juliet (met, had met) at a party.

3. By the time the party was over, they (fell, had fallen) in love.

4. Unfortunately, though, their families (feud, were feuding), so Romeo and Juliet (hid, had hidden) their affection for one another.

5. They secretly (married, had married) and (planned, had planned) to run away together.

6. But long before Juliet met Romeo, Juliet's father (decided, had decided) that she would marry a man named Paris.

7. The night before her wedding, Juliet (took, had taken) a potion that made her appear dead.

8. This tale (has, has had) a tragic ending because before Romeo found Juliet in her tomb, he (was not informed, had not been informed) that she wasn't really dead.

9. So he (committed, had committed) suicide, and Juliet (stabbed, had stabbed) herself when she awoke to find his body.

10. If I read this story again, I (have, will have) a tissue ready to dry

    my tears.

Exercise 6 Choosing Verb Tense

Underline the correct verb form.

1. In the eighteenth century, Benjamin Franklin (is saying, said)

   that compound interest was the "eighth wonder of the world."

2. Today, taking advantage of compound interest (is, was) still one

   way to grow a fortune.

3. I wish I (had, had been) started investing years ago.

4. If I (will have, could have) saved $2,000 per year from age 21

   on, I (would have, would have had) over a million dollars now.

5. I (have, had) never realized this until I did the math.

6. So I (have decided, could have been deciding) to begin investing

   money every month from now on.

7. Yesterday, I (determined, have determined) an amount I should

   save each week.

8. I hope that you (will have considered, are considering) doing

   the same thing.

9. By the time we're ready to retire, we (were, may be)

   millionaires.

10. Someday we (will worry, worried) about how to pay the bills.

Exercise 7 Choosing Verb Tense

Underline the correct verb form.

1. Before the major highways of the postwar period, Highway 66
   (was, is) one of the most important roads in America, linking
   Chicago to Los Angeles.

2. Officially designated *Highway 66* in 1926, the road was
   (constructed/construct) as a two-lane highway with stops in
   places like Tucumcari, New Mexico, and Winslow, Arizona.

3. U.S. 66—its official designation—was (laid, layed) for one
   reason: to connect small-town America to big cities.

4. U.S. 66 also (set, sat) a new standard for ease of transport owing
   to the good weather in states through which it passed.

5. With the new road, farmers (can, could) transport their crops
   and livestock to markets and meat plants in Chicago.

6. So the new road had (rose, risen) out of the social and economic
   needs of a quickly growing population.

7. Thousands of young men during the 1930s (were, are) put to
   work paving the highway, with work completed in 1938.

8. U.S. 66 (brings, brought) hundreds of thousands of people from the Mid- and Southwest to California during the 1930s.

9. The highway had a huge impact on the economy of the towns through which it passed, and even today many of the gas stations, motels, shops, and restaurants (have been, are) still standing.

10. Immortalized in the song "Get Your Kicks on Route 66," the highway (will be, is) an important part of America's history.

Exercise 8   Using Verbs in Sentences

Use each of these words in a sentence of six words or more.

1. *lie, lay* (rest), *lain, laid* _____

   _____

   _____

   _____

2. *sit, sat, set* _____

   _____

   _____

3. *is, was, were* _____

   _____

   _____

4. *do, does* (or *don't, doesn't*) _____

   _____

⌢ Subject-Verb Agreement

The basic principle of **subject-verb agreement** is that if the subject is singular, the verb should be singular, and if the subject is plural, the verb should be plural. There are ten major guidelines to ensure number agreement between subjects and verbs. In the examples under the following guidelines, the correct subjects and verbs are italicized.

1. Do not let words that come between the subject and verb affect agreement.

   - Modifying phrases and clauses frequently come between the subject and verb.

     The various *types* of drama *were* not *discussed.*

     Angela, who is hitting third, *is* the best player.

     The *price* of those shoes *is* too high.

   - Certain prepositions can cause trouble. The following words and phrases are prepositions, not conjunctions: *along with, as well as, besides, in addition to, including,* and *together with.* The words that function as objects of prepositions cannot also be subjects of the sentence.

     The *coach*, along with the players, *protests* the decision.

   - In compound subjects in which one subject is positive and one subject is negative, the verb agrees with the positive subject.

     Phillip, not the other boys, *was* the culprit.

2. Do not let inversions (verb before subject, not the normal order) affect the agreement of subject and verb.

   - Verbs and other words may come before the subject. Do not let them affect the agreement. To understand subject-verb relationships, recast the sentence in normal word order.

     Are Juan and his *sister* at home? (question form)

     Juan and his *sister are* at home. (normal order)

   - A sentence filler is a word that is grammatically independent of other words in the sentence. The most common fillers are *there* and *here.* Even though a sentence filler precedes the verb, it should not be treated as the subject.

     There *are* many *reasons* for his poor work. (The verb *are* agrees with the subject *reasons.*)

3. A singular verb agrees with a singular indefinite pronoun. (See page 127.)

- Most indefinite pronouns are singular.

  Each of the women *is* ready at this time.

  Neither of the women *is* ready at this time.

  One of the children *is* not paying attention.

- Certain indefinite pronouns do not clearly express either a singular or plural number. Agreement, therefore, depends on the meaning of the sentence as indicated by objects of prepositions. These pronouns are *all, any, none,* and *some.*

  All of the melon *was* good.

  All of the melons *were* good.

  None of the pie *is* acceptable.

  None of the pies *are* acceptable.

4. Two or more subjects joined by *and* usually take a plural verb.

   The *captain* and the *sailors were* happy to be ashore.

   The *trees* and *shrubs need* more care.

   - If the parts of a compound subject mean one and the same person or thing, the verb is singular; if the parts mean more than one, the verb is plural.

     The *secretary* and *treasurer is* not present. (one person)

     The *secretary* and the *treasurer are* not present. (more than one person)

   - When *each* or *every* modify singular subjects joined by *and,* the verb is singular.

     Each *boy* and each *girl brings* a donation.

     Each *woman* and *man has asked* the same questions.

5. Alternative subjects—that is, subjects joined by *or, nor, either/ or, neither/nor, not only/but also*—should be handled in the following manner:

   - If the subjects are both singular, the verb is singular.

     Rosa or *Alicia* is responsible.

   - If the subjects are plural, the verb is plural.

     Neither the *students* nor the *teachers were* impressed by his comments.

- If one of the subjects is singular and the other subject is plural, the verb agrees with the nearer subject.

    Either the Garcia *boys* or their *father goes* to the hospital each day.

    Either their *father* or the Garcia *boys go* to the hospital each day.

6. Collective nouns—*team, family, group, crew, gang, class, faculty,* and the like—take a singular verb if the group is considered a unit but a plural verb if the group is considered as a number of individuals.

    The *team is playing* well tonight.

    The *team are getting* dressed. (Here the individuals are acting not as a unit but separately. If you don't like the way this sounds, rewrite the sentence as "The members of the team are getting dressed.")

7. Titles of books, essays, short stories, and plays; a word spoken of as a word; and the names of businesses take a singular verb.

    The Canterbury Tales was written by Geoffrey Chaucer.

    Markle Brothers has a sale this week.

8. Sums of money, distances, and measurements are followed by a singular verb when a unit is meant. They are followed by a plural verb when the individual elements are considered separately.

    Three dollars was the price. (unit)

    Three dollars were lying there. (individual)

    Five years is a long time. (unit)

    The *first five years were* difficult ones. (individual)

9. Be careful of agreement with nouns ending in -*s*. Several nouns ending in -*s* take a singular verb—for example, *aeronautics, civics, economics, ethics, measles, mumps.*

    Mumps is an extremely unpleasant disease.

    Economics is my major field of study.

10. Some nouns have only a plural form and so take only a plural verb—for example, *clothes, fireworks, scissors, pants,* and *glasses.*

    His *glasses are* dusty.

    Mary's *clothes were* stylish and expensive.

Exercise 9 Making Subjects and Verbs Agree

Underline the verb that agrees in number with the subject.

1. "Two Kinds" (is, are) a short story by Amy Tan.

2. My pants (is, are) wrinkled.

3. Twenty pounds (is, are) a lot to lose in one month.

4. Physics (is, are) a difficult subject to master.

5. *60 Minutes* (is, are) a respected television program.

6. Sears (is, are) having a giant sale.

7. The scissors (is, are) very sharp.

8. Five miles (is, are) too far to walk.

9. The class (is, are) stretching their muscles.

10. My dog and my cat (is, are) sleeping on the couch.

Exercise 10 Making Subjects and Verbs Agree

Underline the verb that agrees in number with the subject.

1. New Orleans (is, are) the site of one of the most celebrated

   parties in the United States.

2. Mardi Gras (are, is) now celebrated in many places outside of

   Louisiana.

3. Mardi Gras, which means "Fat Tuesday," (is, are) always

   forty-six days before Easter.

4. But twelve days before that, the crowd (begins, begin) to grow.

5. All of the bands in the state of Louisiana (converges, converge) on New Orleans.

6. A visitor, along with just about all of the city's residents, (enjoys, enjoy) nonstop jazz and blues music.

7. Cajun and Creole food (satisfies, satisfy) the revelers' hungry appetites.

8. There (is, are) numerous parades, but the best ones (occurs, occur) during the last five days of the celebration.

9. Each of the spectacular parade floats (is, are) decorated and (carries, carry) riders wearing costumes.

10. Four miles (is, are) the length of a typical parade route.

11. Beads, coins, cups, and an occasional medallion (is, are) tossed from the floats into the crowd.

12. People who line the parade route (tries, try) to catch as many trinkets as they can.

13. One float, the best of all of that parade's floats, (wins, win) an award.

14. Some of the most popular festivities, besides a good parade, (is, are) the masked balls.

15. Every one of the costumes (is, are) outrageous and unique.

16. *Cajun Mardi Gras Masks* (is, are) a book that will give you

    some ideas.

17. The celebration (is, are) a happening of fun and frenzy.

18. After dark, there (is, are) fireworks in the night sky.

19. Neither the participants nor the curious onlooker (wants,

    want) the party to end.

20. (Is, Are) these days of merrymaking something you'd enjoy?

～ Consistency in Tense

Consider this statement:

> We went (1) downtown, and then we watch (2) a movie. Later we
> met (3) some friends from school, and we all go (4) to the mall.
> For most of the evening, we play (5) video games in arcades. It
> was (6) a typical but rather uneventful summer day.

Does the shifting verb tense (to say nothing about the lack of development of ideas) bother you? It should! The writer makes several
unnecessary changes. Verbs 1, 3, and 6 are in the past tense, and
verbs 2, 4, and 5 are in the present tense. Changing all verbs to the
past tense makes the statement much smoother.

> We went downtown, and then we watched a movie. Later we
> met some friends from school, and we all went to the mall. For
> most of the evening, we played video games in arcades. It was a
> typical but rather uneventful summer day.

In other instances you might want to maintain a consistent
present tense. The rules for selecting a tense for a certain kind of
writing are flexible, but you should be consistent, changing tense
only for a good reason.

The present tense is customarily used in writing about literature, even if the literature was written long in the past:

> *Moby Dick* is a novel about Captain Ahab's obsession with a
> great white whale. Ahab *sets* sail with a full crew of sailors who

think they *are going* on merely another whaling voyage. Most of the crew *are* experienced seamen.

The past tense is likely to serve you best in writing about your personal experiences and about historical events (although the present tense can often be used effectively to establish the feeling of intimacy and immediacy):

> In the summer of 1991, Hurricane Bob *hit* the Atlantic coast region. It *came* ashore near Cape Hatteras and *moved* north. The winds *reached* a speed of more than ninety miles per hour on Cape Cod but then *slackened* by the time Bob reached Maine.

Exercise 11   Making Verbs Consistent in Tense

Change the verbs in the following paragraph as necessary to maintain a mostly consistent past tense.

(1) Tarzan spoke to Jane in simple language. (2) His most famous words were "Me Tarzan, you Jane." (3) Before the arrival of Jane, there are only jungle friends for Tarzan. (4) Those animals seldom used the full eight parts of speech. (5) For example, lions seldom utter verbs. (6) Elephants had no patience with prepositions. (7) Chimps condemn conjunctions. (8) Their punctuation was replaced largely by snarls, growls, and breast-beating. (9) Their language is well-suited to Tarzan. (10) To him, jungle language was like swinging on a vine. (11) A one-syllable yell is a full oration. (12) Jane never ridiculed his grammar or even his yelling. (13) She holds back criticism of the king of the apes. (14) Despite their difference in language skills, they establish hut

keeping. (15) They were very poor and wore simple garments made of skins. (16) Their main transportation is well-placed hanging vines. (17) Tarzan and Jane had a child. (18) They name him "Boy." (19) Fortunately, they did not have another male child. (20) Such an occurrence could have caused a language gridlock.

Exercise 12   Making Verbs Consistent in Tense

Change the verbs in the following paragraph as necessary to maintain a mostly consistent past tense.

(1) Many unique foods have been introduced over the years, but none, perhaps, is as historically important and quintessentially American as Spam®. 2) Hormel develops its new product in 1937. (3) Jay C. Hormel, son of Hormel founder George A. Hormel, is instrumental in creating what was then called "Hormel Spiced Ham." (4) Spam will be made of ham and pork shoulder. (5) It was the first meat product that did not need refrigeration—a fact that makes it an amazing convenience food. (6) The new product will be so popular that other meat packers copied the idea, and Hormel is starting to lose market share. (7) Hormel had a brilliant idea to have a contest to come up with a new name for its tasty canned meat. (8) The winner of the contest will be receiving $100 for coining the name Spam, and the

rest is history. (9) In 1937, Spam was advertised heavily as "the

Miracle Meat." (10) Hormel sponsors a radio show with popular

comedians George Burns and Gracie Allen and introducing a new

character, Spammy the Pig. (11) During World War II, Spam is

used extensively by the military. (12) Nikita Khrushchev will

say that Spam keeps the Russian Army alive during the war.

(13) This amazing product was a staple of people living in

Allied countries and occupied areas during the war. (14) Many

Americans enjoyed Spam frequently because it was not rationed

as beef is. (15) Having grown up during the war years in

England, where Spam is a staple food, the members of the comedy

group Monty Python later immortalize Spam in one of its most

famous sketches. (16) After the 1950s, Spam continues to be

improved and enjoyed. (17) Consumers are offered smoke-flavored

Spam in 1971, and low-salt Spam will become available in 1986.

(18) SPAM Lite was introduced in the early 1990s. (19) Spam is a

favorite among many Pacific Islanders who first tasted this treat

during World War II. (20) More than sixty years after its first

appearance on store shelves, millions around the world heartily

agreed that "Cold or hot, Spam hits the spot!"

Exercise 13   Making Verbs Consistent in Tense

Change the verbs in the following paragraph as necessary to main-tain a mostly consistent past tense.

(1) Once upon a time, a Professor Glen was very popular with his students. (2) He kept long office hours and always speaks nicely to his students on campus. (3) He even brought popcorn for them to munch on during tests. (4) Respecting their sensitivity, he marks with a soothing green ink instead of red. (5) He often told jokes and listened attentively to their complaints about assignments. (6) The leaders of student government elect him teacher of the century. (7) Who would not admire such a person? (8) Then late one semester, a strange and shocking thing happens. (9) Everywhere there were students in despair. (10) Professor Glen no longer speaks openly to students. (11) During his office hours, he locked his door and posted a pit bull. (12) He corrects student papers in flaming scarlet. (13) Instead of popcorn, he gave them hot scorn. (14) He told no more jokes and sneered at their complaints about assignments. (15) He sticks out his tongue at students on campus. (16) He offered good grades for cash. (17) Professor Glen even accepts Visa cards and validated parking. (18) One day the students heard a thumping sound in a classroom closet. (19) Looking inside, they find the true Professor Glen. (20) The other one was an evil twin professor.

Exercise 14   Making Verbs Consistent in Tense

Correct verbs as needed in the following paragraph to achieve consistency in tense.

Guam is located in the Mariana chain of islands. It is first inhabited by the Chamorro people. This island is a U.S. Trust Territory since 1898, when the Spanish give up control after losing the Spanish-American War. The Japanese occupy the island during World War II until it is recaptured by the United States in July 1944. Today the island was a popular tourist spot for Asians as well as being a site for several U.S. military bases. A beautiful tropical island, Guam looked much like the Hawaiian Islands. The original inhabitants come from Indonesia around 4,000 years ago. From those times came the belief in Taotao Mona, spirits of the ancient Chamorros; today most residents of Guam were Christian. People born in Guam are American citizens. In fact, the motto of Guam was "Where America's Day Begins."

⌒ Active and Passive Voice

Which of these sentences sounds better to you?

Andre Ethier slammed a home run.
A home run was slammed by Andre Ethier.

Both sentences carry the same message, but the first expresses it more effectively. The subject (*Andre Ethier*) is the actor. The verb (*slammed*) is the action. The direct object (*home run*) is the receive of the action. The second sentence lacks the vitality of the first because the receiver of the action is the subject; the doer is embedded in the prepositional phrase at the end of the sentence.

The first sentence demonstrates the active voice. It has an active verb (one that leads to a direct object), and the action moves from the beginning to the end of the sentence. The second exhibits the passive voice (with the action reflecting back on the subject). When given a choice, you should usually select the active voice. It promotes energy and directness.

The passive voice, though not usually the preferred form, does have its uses:

- When the doer of the action is unknown or unimportant

  My car was stolen. (The doer, a thief, is unknown.)

- When the receiver of the action is more important than the doer

  My neighbor was permanently disabled by an irresponsible drunk driver. (The neighbor's suffering, not the drunk driver, is the focus.)

As you can see, the passive construction places the doer at the end of a prepositional phrase (as in the second example) or does not include the doer in the statement at all (as in the first example). Instead, the passive voice places the receiver of the action in the subject position, and it presents the verb in its past-tense form preceded by a *to be* helper. The transformation is a simple one:

ACTIVE   Boris read the book.

PASSIVE   The book was read by Boris.

Weak sentences often involve the unnecessary and ineffective use of the passive form.

<hr />

Exercise 15   Using Active and Passive Voice

Rewrite these sentences to convert the verbs from passive to active voice.

A letter has been written by me to you.

ᴀ honest dollar was never made by his ancestors.

3. The assignment was approved by the instructor.

4. The instructor was given a much-deserved medal of valor by the president of the student body.

5. Few people noticed that most of the work was done by the quiet students.

6. The ballgame was interrupted by bats catching flies in the outfield.

7. The commotion at the apathy convention was caused by a person who attended.

8. The air was filled with speeches by him.

9. He doesn't have an enemy, but he is hated by all his friends.

10. His lips are never passed by a lie—he talks through his nose.

⌇ Strong Verbs

Because the verb is an extremely important part of any sentence, it should be chosen with care. Some of the most widely used verbs are the *being* verbs: *is, was, were, are, am*. We couldn't get along in English without them, but writers often use them when more forceful and effective verbs are available.

Consider these examples:

WEAK VERB   Regina *is* the leader of the race.
STRONG VERB   Regina *leads* in the race.
WEAK VERB   Regina *was* the first to finish.
STRONG VERB   Regina *finished* first.

Exercise 16 Using Strong Verbs

Replace the weak verbs with stronger ones in the following sentences. Delete unnecessary words to make each sentence even more concise if you can.

1. My watch is running slowly.

2. My computer is quite inexpensive.

3. The horse was a fast runner.

4. They were writers who wrote well.

5. The dog is sleeping on the bed.

6. Mr. Hawkins is a real estate salesperson.

7. José is in attendance at Santa Ana College.

8. This assignment is something I like.

9. We are the successful students here.

10. She is in the process of combing her hair.

Exercise 17 Using Strong Verbs

Replace the weak verbs with stronger ones in the following sentences. Delete unnecessary words to make each sentence even more concise if you can.

1. Babe Ruth was the hitter of many home runs.

2. The chef was a man with a fondness for food.

3. To graduate in two years is my plan.

4. John Hancock was the first signer of the Declaration of

   Independence.

5. Juanita is the organizer of the event.

6. Cooking is something she likes to do.

7. Veronica was the owner of the restaurant.

8. Tung will be the winner of the tournament.

9. They were in love with each other.

10. His passion for her was in a state of demise.

〰️ Chapter Review

Exercise 18   Correcting Verb Problems

Correct problems with verb form, tense, agreement, strength, and voice. As a summary of a novel, this piece should be mostly in the present tense.

Summary of *The Old Man and the Sea*

Santiago, one of many local fishermen, have not caught a fish in eighty-four days. Young Manolin, despite the objections of his parents, has a belief in the old man. His parents says Santiago is un-lucky, and they will not let their son go fishing with him.

The next day, Santiago sit sail. Soon he catch a small tuna, which he used for bait. Then a huge marlin hit the bait with a strike. The old man cannot rise the fish to the surface, and it pulled the boat through-out the rest of the day and during the night.

During the second day, Santiago's hand is injured by the line and he become extremely tired, but he holds on. When the fish moves to the surface, Santiago notes that it was two feet longer than his skiff. It is the biggest fish he has ever saw. He thinks in wonder if he will be up to the task of catching it. With the line braced across his shoulders, he sleeped for a while. As he dreams gloriously of lions and porpoises and of being young, he is awaken by the fish breaking water again, and Santiago is sure the fish is tiring. He lays in the boat and waits.

On the third day, the fish came to the surface. Santiago pull steadily on the line, and finally it is harpooned and killed by Santiago. The fish is tied to the skiff by him. But sharks attacked and mutilate the huge marlin. Using an oar, he beats on the sharks courageously with all his strength, but they strips the fish to a skeleton.

With the bones still tied to the skiff, the exhausted old man returned to shore. Other fishermen and tourists marvel at the eighteen-foot skeleton of the fish as the old man lays asleep. The young boy knew he has much to learn from the old man and is determined to go fishing with him.

8

Pronouns

Should you say, "Between you and *I*" or "Between you and *me*"? What about "Let's you and *I* do this" or "Let's you and *me* do this"? Are you confused about when to use *who* and *whom*? Is it "Everyone should wear *their* coat," or "*his* coat," or "*his or her* coat"? Is there anything wrong with saying, "When *you* walk down the streets of Laredo"?

The examples in the first paragraph represent the most common problems many people have with pronouns. This chapter will help you identify the standard forms and understand why they are correct. For you, the result should be expertise and confidence.

∼ Pronoun Case

Case is the form a pronoun takes as it fills a position in a sentence. Words such as *you* and *it* do not change, but others do, and they change in predictable ways. For example, *I* is a subject word and *me* is an object word. As you refer to yourself, you will select a pronoun that fits a certain part of sentence structure. You say, "*I* will write the paper," not "*Me* will write the paper," because *I* is in the subject position. But you say, "She will give the apple to *me*," not "She will give the apple to *I*" because *me* is in the object position. These are pronouns that do change:

Subject	Object
I	me
he	him
she	her
we	us
they	them
who, whoever	whom, whomever

Subjective Case

Person	Singular	Plural
First	I	we
Second	you	you
Third	he she it	they
	who	

Subjective pronouns can fill two positions in a sentence.

1. Pronouns in the subjective case may fill subject positions.
   a. Some subjective pronouns will be easy to identify because they are at the beginning of the sentence.

   I dance in the park.

   He dances in the park.

   She dances in the park.

   We dance in the park.

   They dance in the park.

   Who is dancing in the park?

   b. Others will be more difficult to identify because they are not at the beginning of a sentence and may not appear to be part of a clause. The words *than* and *as* are signals for these special arrangements, which can be called incompletely stated clauses.

   He is taller than *I* (am).

   She is younger than *we* (are).

   We work as hard as *they* (do).

   The words *am, are,* and *do,* which complete the clauses, have been omitted. We are actually saying, "He is taller than *I am,*" "She is younger than *we are,*" and "We work as hard as *they do.*" The italicized pronouns are subjects of "understood" verbs.

2. Pronouns in the subjective case may refer back to the subject.

a. They may follow a form of the verb *to be,* such as *was, were, are, am,* and *is.*

I believe it is *he.*

It was *she* who spoke.

The victims were *they.*

b. Some nouns and pronouns refer back to an earlier noun without referring back through the verb.

The leading candidates—Juan, Darnelle, Steve, Kimlieu, and *I*—made speeches.

Objective Case

Person	Singular	Plural
First	me	us
Second	you	you
Third	him her it	them

whom

Objective pronouns can also fill two positions in sentences.

1. Pronouns in the objective case may fill object positions.

a. They may be objects after the verb. A direct object answers the question *What?* or *Whom?* in connection with the verb.

We brought *it* to your house. (*What* did we bring? *it*)

We saw *her* in the library (*Whom* did we see? *her*)

An indirect object answers the question *to whom* in connection with the verb.

I gave *him* the message. (*To whom* did I give the message? *to him*)

The doctor told *us* the test results. (*To whom* did the doctor tell the results? *to us*)

b. They may be objects after prepositions.

The problem was clear to *us*.

I offered the opportunity to Steve and *him*.

2. Object pronouns may also refer back to object words.

They gave the results to us—Judy and *me*.

The judge addressed the defendants—John and *her*.

Techniques for Determining Case

Here are three techniques that will help you decide which pronoun to use when the choice seems difficult:

1. If you have a compound element (such as a subject or an object of a preposition), consider only the pronoun part. The sound alone will probably tell you the answer.

She gave the answer to Marie and (I, me).

Marie and the pronoun make up a compound object of the preposition *to*. Disregard the noun, *Marie*, and ask yourself, "Would I say, 'She gave the answer *to me* or *to I*'?" The way the words sound would tell you the answer is *to me*. Of course, if you immediately notice that the pronoun is in an object position, you need not bother with sound.

2. If you are choosing between *who* (subject word) and *whom* (object word), look to the right to see if the next verb has a subject. If it does not, the pronoun probably is the subject, but if it does, the pronoun probably is an object.

A related technique works the same way. If the next important word after *who* or *whom* in a statement is a noun or pronoun, the correct word will usually be *whom*. However, if the next important word is not a noun or pronoun, the correct word will be *who*.

To apply these techniques, you must disregard qualifier clauses such as "I think," "it seems," and "we hope."

The person (*who*, whom) works hardest will win. (*Who* is the correct answer because it is the subject of the verb *works*.)

The person (who, *whom*) we admire most is José. (*Whom* is the correct answer because the next verb, *admire*, already has a subject, *we*. *Whom* is an object.)

Amanda is the person (*who*, whom), we hope, has won. (*We hope* is a qualifier clause, so we disregard it. Because we need a subject for the verb *has won*, we select the subject word *who*.)

3. *Let's* is made up of the words *let* and *us* and means "you *let us*"; therefore, when you select a pronoun to follow it, consider the two original words and select another object word—*me*.

Let's you and (I, *me*) take a trip to Westwood. (Think of "You let us, you and me, take a trip to Westwood." *Us* and *me* are object words.)

Exercise 1 Selecting Pronouns

Underline the correct pronouns.

1. (Who, Whom) does not love to chew gum—at least sometimes?

2. By (who, whom) was the first chewing gum invented?

3. (Whoever, Whomever) invented this treat did us all a favor.

4. The ancient Greeks, (who, whom) invented democracy, also invented a type of gum called *mastiche* made from tree resin.

5. The ancient Mayans, of (who, whom) many have heard, chewed *chicle,* the sap of the *sapodilla* tree.

6. Early American settlers and North American Indians, both of (who, whom) chewed gum made of sap from spruce trees, can be counted among this confection's originators.

7. John B. Curtis, (who, whom) is credited with the sale of the first commercial gum in 1848, made a product called State of Maine Pure Spruce gum.

8. In 1869, Antonio Lopez de Santa Anna first showed
   Thomas Adams—(who, whom) later invented a machine to
   manufacture gum—the wonder of *chicle.*

9. (Whoever, Whomever) loves Dentyne owes a debt of gratitude
   to its inventor, a New York druggist by the name of Franklin V.
   Canning.

10. In 1906 Frank Fleer, (who, whom) we must never forget,
    invented bubble gum, which he called Blibber-Blubber gum.

Exercise 2   Selecting Pronouns

Underline the correct pronouns.

1. (She, Her) and (I, me) went to the Ripley's Believe It or Not
   Museum.

2. (We, Us) young people are fascinated by the weird, the gross,
   and the creepy.

3. I would rather go to the museum with you than with (she, her).

4. There are those (who, whom) would urge you not to waste
   your money to see oddities like shrunken heads and a portrait
   of John Wayne made of dryer lint.

5. Robert L. Ripley, an eccentric newspaper cartoonist (who,
   whom) loved to travel, collected strange things.

6. He is the man (who, whom) we can thank for acquiring many of the artifacts now housed in forty-four "Odditoriums" in ten different countries.

7. (Who, Whom) wouldn't be entertained by a stuffed six-legged cow or pictures of two-headed lambs and other freaks of nature?

8. And don't forget the bizarre videos, like the one of a man (who, whom) swallows and then regurgitates a live mouse.

9. I feel sorry for (whoever, whomever) misses the replica of the "Mona Lisa" made of croutons.

10. Just between you and (I, me), though, the wax figures of bizarre accident victims, like the man impaled on a crowbar, were a little unnerving.

Exercise 3 Selecting Pronouns

Underline the correct pronouns.

1. Let's you and (I, me) consider some stories called urban legends.

2. These are stories heard by people like you and (I, me), which are passed on as if they were true.

3. We hear them from people (who, whom) have heard them from others.

4. You have probably heard more of them than (I, me), but I'll tell some anyway.

5. One is about a guard dog named Gork (who, whom) was found choking in his owner's bedroom.

6. The owner, (who, whom) loved Gork dearly, took him to the veterinarian, left him, and headed home.

7. While driving home, the owner answered his cell phone, asking "To (who, whom) am I speaking?"

8. "This is your vet calling. Just between you and (I, me), you have a big problem here."

9. "Gork has someone's detached finger stuck in his throat, and I've called the police, (who, whom) are on their way to your house."

10. Eventually the police arrested an angry armed man (who, whom) they suspected had broken into the owner's house, where Gork had bitten off and choked on the intruder's finger while the intruder, (who, whom) had crawled into a closet, passed out from loss of blood.

Exercise 4   Selecting Pronouns

Underline the correct pronouns.

1. (We, Us) students of Indian history are amazed by the life of Geronimo or *Goyathlay*—his Indian name, meaning "one who yawns."

2. In 1886, (he, him) and a small band of followers were the last American Indians to surrender to the U.S. Army.

3. Technically never a chief, (he, him) became a medicine man, a spiritual leader to the Chiricahua Apache in what is now New Mexico.

4. Geronimo was famous for his daring raids on Mexicans when he led his warriors against (they, them) during his time in Sonora.

5. It was (they, them), the Mexicans, who gave Goyathlay the nickname, Geronimo.

6. Most who fought against him knew that he was a better warrior than (they, them).

7. Geronimo plotted revenge against those of European ancestry after Spanish troops from Mexico killed his wife and children while (he, him) was away from home on a trading excursion.

8. After this event, he for (who, whom) there was so much sadness, began attacking Mexican settlements with great ferocity.

9. After 1876 when the Chiricahua Apache were forced to live on a reservation in the dry wasteland of eastern Arizona, Geronimo led his followers into Mexico to escape what (they, them) considered imprisonment on the reservation.

10. Amazingly, Geronimo became a mainstream celebrity because of

his exploits, and it was (he, him) who became a rancher and rode

in the inaugural parade of President Theodore Roosevelt in 1905.

～ Pronoun-Antecedent Agreement

Every pronoun refers to an earlier noun, the **antecedent** of the
pronoun, which is the noun that the pronoun replaces. The pronoun brings the reader back to the earlier thought. Here are some
examples:

> I tried to buy *tickets* for the concert, but *they* were all sold.
>
> *Roger* painted a picture of a pickup truck. *It* was so good that *he*
> entered *it* in an art show.

A pronoun agrees with its antecedent in person, number, and
gender. **Person**—first, second, or third—indicates perspective, or
point of view. **Number** indicates singular or plural. **Gender** indicates
sex: masculine, feminine, or neuter.

Subject Words			*Object Words*		
Person	**Singular**	**Plural**	**Person**	**Singular**	**Plural**
First	I	we	**First**	me	us
Second	you	you	**Second**	you	you
Third	he, she, it	they	**Third**	him, her, it	them

Agreement in Person

Avoid needless shifting in person, which means shifting of point of
view, such as from *I* to *you*. The following paragraph is an example of
an inconsistent point of view. See if you can tell where the shifts occur.

INCONSISTENT   The wedding did not go well. It was a
disaster. *You* could see the trouble develop
when the caterers started serving drinks
before the ceremony. Then the bride
started arguing with her future mother-in-
law. *I* was ready to leave right away. After that, the sound system went out and

the band canceled. *You* wished *you* hadn't come, but *you* had to stay. *I* will never forget that day.

The word *you* is second-person point of view; the word *I* is first person. When the writer switches back and forth, the result is reader confusion and annoyance. The following revision corrects the problem by making the point of view consistently first person.

CONSISTENT   The wedding did not go well. It was a disaster. *I* could see the trouble develop when the caterers started serving drinks before the ceremony. Then the bride started arguing with her future mother-in-law. *I* was ready to leave right away. After that, the sound system went out and the band canceled. *I* wished *I* hadn't come, but *I* had to stay. *I* will never forget that day.

Agreement in Number

Most problems with pronoun-antecedent agreement involve number. The principles are simple: If the antecedent (the word the pronoun refers back to) is singular, use a singular pronoun. If the antecedent is plural, use a plural pronoun.

1. A singular antecedent requires a singular pronoun.

   Riley forgot *his* notebook.

2. A plural antecedent requires a plural pronoun.

   Many *students* cast *their* votes today.

3. A singular indefinite pronoun as an antecedent takes a singular pronoun. Most indefinite pronouns are singular. The following are common indefinite singular pronouns: *anybody, anyone, each, either, everybody, everyone, no one, nobody, one, somebody, someone.*

   Each of the girls brought *her* book.

4. A plural indefinite pronoun as an antecedent takes a plural pronoun.

   Few knew *their* assignments.

5. Certain indefinite pronouns do not clearly express either a singular or plural number. Agreement, therefore, depends on the meaning of the sentence as indicated by the object of the preposition. These pronouns are *all, any, none,* and *some.*

   All of the melon *was* good.

   All of the melons *were* good.

   None of the pie *is* acceptable.

   None of the pies *are* acceptable.

6. Two or more antecedents, singular or plural, take a plural pronoun. Such antecedents are usually joined by *and* or by commas and *and.*

   Max and his *parents* bought *their* presents early.

   The *players, team owner,* and *fans* expressed *their* views.

7. Alternate antecedents—that is, antecedents joined by *or, nor, whether/or, either/or, neither/nor, not only/but also*—require a pronoun that agrees with the nearer antecedent.

   Neither Igor nor his *friends* lost *their* way.

   Neither his friends nor *Igor* lost *his* way.

8. In a sentence with the expression *one of*, the antecedent is usually the plural noun that follows.

   He is one of those *people who* want *their* money now.

9. In a sentence with the expression *only one of*, the antecedent is usually the singular word *one.*

   Alexandra is the *only one of* the members *who* wants *her* money now.

10. When collective nouns such as *team, jury, committee,* and *band* are used as antecedents, they take a singular pronoun if they are considered as units.

    The *jury* is doing *its* [not *their*] best.

    When individual behavior is suggested, collective nouns take a plural form.

    The *jury* are putting on *their* coats.

11. The words *each, every,* and *many a(n)* before a noun make the noun singular.

> *Each child* and *adult* was *his* or *her* own authority.
>
> *Each* and *every person* doubted *himself* or *herself.*
>
> *Many a* person is capable of knowing *himself* or *herself.*

Agreement in Gender

The pronoun should agree with its antecedent in gender, if the gender of the antecedent is specific. Masculine and feminine pronouns are gender-specific: *he, him, she, her.* Others are neuter: *I, we, me, us, it, they, them, who, whom, that, which.* The words *who* and *whom* refer to people. *That* can refer to ideas, things, and people, although usually not to people. *Which* refers to ideas and things; it never refers to people.

> My *girlfriend* gave me *her* best advice. (feminine)
>
> Mighty *Casey* tried *his* best. (masculine)
>
> The *people with whom* I work are loud. (neuter)

Indefinite singular pronouns used as antecedents require, of course, singular pronouns. Handling the gender of these singular pronouns is not as obvious; opinion is divided.

1. Traditionally, writers have used the masculine form of pronouns to refer to the indefinite singular pronouns when the gender is unknown.

   > *Everyone* should work until *he* drops.

2. The use of the masculine form of pronouns alone, however, suggests a sex bias. To avoid a perceived sex bias, most writers prefer to use *he or she* or *his or her* instead of just *he* or *his.*

   > *Everyone* should work until *he or she* drops.

3. Although option 1 is less cumbersome, it is offensive and illogical to many listeners and readers, and option 2 used several times in a short passage can be awkward. To avoid those possible problems, writers often use plural forms.

   > *All people* should work until *they* drop.

In any case, avoid using a plural pronoun with a singular indefinite pronoun; such usage violates the basic principle of number agreement.

INCORRECT   *Everyone* should do *their* best.

Exercise 5 Selecting Pronouns: Person, Gender, and Number

Correct the faulty pronouns for problems in person, gender, and number.

1. The people who were called Vikings lived between 800 and 1100 CE.

2. Most have heard the term "Viking" but you may not know that the word comes from an Old Norse verb, "vika" meaning "to go off."

3. Each and every Viking could count what is now Denmark, Sweden, or Norway as their original homeland.

4. In the early years, Vikings only left his or her home during the warm months to explore and exploit relatively close lands, such as coastal France and England.

5. Later, Vikings developed permanent bases who were away from home to facilitate trade and conquest in areas as far as the Middle East, the Baltic, and North America.

6. Vikings were fierce warriors that conquered England and colonized Iceland and Greenland.

7. Originally the Vikings believed in gods such as Odin, Thor, and Frey, which lived in an eternal and heroic struggle with forces of the universe, but in the late 900s the Vikings converted to Christianity.

8. People throughout much of what is now Western Europe had his or her lives—either through trading or war—affected by Vikings.

9. The Viking period has left their continued influence in hundreds of English words.

10. These fearsome people of the North were able to maintain his or her political independence largely because no one could conquer them.

Exercise 6 Selecting Pronouns: Person, Gender, and Number
Underline the correct pronoun for person, gender, and number.

1. The band always ends (its, their) concert with a lively tuba solo.

2. Every American should save money, or (they, he or she) may not have enough for retirement.

3. Each camper must bring (their, his or her) own shaving cream.

4. If the class doesn't go on the field trip, (it, they) will miss the mummy exhibit.

5. Each of those farmers knows that (he, they) must rotate (his, their) crops.

6. Pauline and Reggie left (their, his or her) hearts in San Francisco.

7. Everyone should leave (their, his or her) world a better place.

8. Neither the bride nor the bridesmaids could control (her, their) giggles during the ceremony.

9. He is one of those men who likes to drive (his, their) car fast.

10. Every rose has (its, their) thorn, every dog has (its, his or her) day, and every cloud has (its, his or her) silver lining.

〜 Pronoun Reference

A pronoun must refer clearly to its antecedent. Because a pronoun is a substitute word, it can express meaning clearly and definitely only if its antecedent is easily identified.

In some sentence constructions, gender and number make the reference clear.

> Cliff and Martina discussed *his* absences and *her* good attendance. (gender)
>
> If the three older boys in the *club* carry out those plans, *it* will break up. (number)

Avoid ambiguous reference. The following sentences illustrate the kind of confusion that results from structuring sentences with more than one possible antecedent for the pronoun.

UNCLEAR   Brady gave Owen *his* money and clothes.

CLEAR   Brady gave his own money and clothes to Owen.

UNCLEAR   Kylie told her sister that *her* car had a flat tire.

CLEAR   Kylie said to her sister, "Your car has a flat tire."

When using a pronoun to refer to a general idea, make sure that the reference is clear. The pronouns used frequently in this way are *this, that, which,* and *it.* The best solution may be to recast the sentence to omit the pronoun in question.

UNCLEAR Molly whistled the same tune over and over, *which* irritated me.

CLEAR Molly whistled the same tune over and over, a *habit* that irritated me.

RECAST Her whistling the same tune over and over irritated me.

Exercise 7 Selecting Pronouns: Reference and Agreement

Correct the problems in pronoun reference and agreement.

1. Running as a competitive sport has a long history, but none longer than that of the event known as the marathon which is amazing.

2. The first running of this "event" took place in 490 BCE at the Battle of Marathon, and it is still discussed today.

3. A Greek soldier named Pheidippides ran from the battle site near the town of Marathon to Athens with the news of a great victory over the Persians which led to a celebration.

4. It says in the legend, that after delivering the great news, Pheidippides collapsed and died.

5. The modern Marathon was first run in 1896 at the first modern Olympics in Athens, but they only had twenty-five contestants to run the 24.85-mile course.

6. At the 1908 Olympic Games in London, they changed the length of the race to 26 miles and 385 yards, so the runners could go from Windsor Castle to the stadium and pass in front of the royal viewing box.

7. Finally they standardized the length of the race at 26.2 miles for the 1924 games in Paris.

8. Runners who compete in the Marathon typically train by running 100 miles a week while eating special diets and doing weight training for upper-body strength which takes real dedication.

9. It says in some sources that the Marathon is the most grueling Olympic event.

10. Because of its historical importance, they always hold the running of the Marathon on the last day of the Olympics.

∽ Chapter Review

Exercise 8   Writing Sentences with Correct Pronouns

Write a sentence using each of the following words. Do not use the word as the first one in the sentence. One sentence should contain the word between *before a pronoun, such as "Between you and _____," and one sentence should contain the contraction* let's *before a pronoun, such as "Let's you and _____."*

1. she _____

_____

_____

2. her _____

_____

_____

3. him _____

_____

_____

4. us _____

_____

_____

5. who _____

_____

_____

6. whom _____

_____

_____

7. me _____

_____

_____

8. I _____

_____

_____

9. they _____

_____

_____

10. them _____

_____

_____

9

Adjectives and Adverbs

Adjectives modify (describe) nouns and pronouns and answer the questions *Which one? What kind?* and *How many?*

WHICH ONE?   The <u>new</u> <u>car</u> is mine.
                      adj n

WHAT KIND?   <u>Mexican</u> <u>food</u> is my favorite.
                 adj   n

HOW MANY?   A <u>few</u> <u>friends</u> are all one needs.
                adj   n

Adverbs modify verbs, adjectives, or other adverbs and answer the questions *How? Where? When?* and *Why?* Most words ending in *-ly* are adverbs.

WHERE?   The cuckoo <u>flew</u> <u>south</u>.
                v   adv

WHEN?   The cuckoo <u>flew</u> <u>yesterday</u>.
               v   adv

WHY?   The cuckoo <u>flew</u> <u>because of the cold weather.</u>
               v   adv phrase

HOW?   The cuckoo <u>flew</u> <u>swiftly</u>.
              v   adv

<u>Without adjectives and adverbs,</u> <u>even</u> John Steinbeck, the *<u>famous</u>*
      adv phrase   adv   adj

<u>Nobel Prize–winning</u> author, <u>surely</u> could <u>not</u> have described the
      adj   adv   adv

<u>crafty</u> octopus <u>so</u> <u>well</u>,
 adj   adv adv

136

Exercise 1 Using Adjectives and Adverbs

This excerpt is from John Steinbeck's novel Cannery Row. *Before you read the paragraph that follows the excerpt, fill in the blanks for the adjectives and adverbs that have been omitted in this exercise.*

(1) _____ the (2) _____ murderer, the octopus, steals

(3) _____, (4) _____, (5) _____, moving like a

(6) _____ mist, pretending (7) _____ to be a bit of

weed, (8) _____ a rock, (9) _____ a lump of

(10) _____ meat while its (11) _____ eyes watch

(12) _____. It oozes and flows toward a (13) _____

crab, and as it comes close its (14) _____ eyes burn and its

body turns (15) _____ with the (16) _____ color of

anticipation and rage. (17) _____, (18) _____, it runs

(19) _____ on the tips of its arms, as (20) _____ as a

(21) _____ cat. It leaps (22) _____ on the crab, there is

a puff of (23) _____ fluid, and the (24) _____ mass is

obscured in the (25) _____ cloud while the octopus murders

the crab.

Of course, Steinbeck vividly depicts his subject through his skillful choice of nouns such as *murderer* and *rage*, and of verbs such as *steals*, *oozes*, *flows*, *burn*, *runs*, and *leaps*, but the absence of adjectives and adverbs eliminates a whole dimension of expression. The missing adjectives and adverbs are the following: (1) Then, (2) creeping, (3) out, (4) slowly, (5) softly, (6) gray, (7) now, (8) now, (9) now, (10) decaying, (11) evil, (12) coldly, (13) feeding, (14) yellow, (15) rosy, (16) pulsing,

(17) Then, (18) suddenly, (19) lightly, (20) ferociously, (21) charging, (22) savagely, (23) black, (24) struggling, (25) sepia.

We have two concerns regarding the use of adjectives and adverbs in writing. One is a matter of diction, or word choice—in this case, how to select adjectives and adverbs that will strengthen the writing. The other is how to identify and correct problems with these modifiers.

∿ Selecting Adjectives and Adverbs

If you want to finish the sentence "She danced _____," you have many adverbs to select from, including these:

bewitchingly	angelically	quaintly	zestfully
gracefully	grotesquely	carnally	smoothly
divinely	picturesquely	serenely	unevenly

If you want to finish the sentence "She was a(n) _____ speaker," you have another large selection, this time of adjectives such as the following:

distinguished	dependable	effective	sly
influential	impressive	polished	astute
adequate	boring	abrasive	humorous

Adjectives and adverbs can be used to enhance communication. If you have a thought, you know what it is, but when you deliver that thought to someone else, you may not say or write what you mean. Your thought may be eloquent and your word choice weak. Keep in mind that no two words mean exactly the same thing. Further, some words are vague or general. If you settle for a common word such as *good* or a slang word such as *neat* to characterize something that you like, you will be limiting your communication. Of course, those who know you best may understand fairly well; after all, certain people who are really close may be able to convey ideas using only grunts and gestures.

But what if you want to write to someone you hardly know to explain how you feel about an important issue? Then the more precise the word, the better the communication. By using modifiers, you may be able to add significant information. Anything can be overdone, however, so use adjectives and adverbs wisely and economically.

Your first resource in searching for more effective adjectives should be your own vocabulary storehouse. Another resource is a good thesaurus (book of synonyms). Finally, you may want to collaborate with others to discuss and share ideas.

Exercise 2 Using Adjectives

Provide adjectives to modify these nouns, using a dictionary, a thesaurus, or the resources designated by your instructor. Use only single words, not adjective phrases.

1. A(n) _____ dog ignored the cat.

2. A(n) _____ comedian waited for applause.

3. A(n) _____ voice cried out in the night.

4. A(n) _____ neighbor turned up his boom box.

5. A(n) _____ ballplayer never gives up.

6. A(n) _____ party occurs only in one's imagination.

7. A(n) _____ singer sang off key.

8. A(n) _____ date waited at the club.

9. A(n) _____ car careened down the street.

10. A(n) _____ job is hard to find.

Exercise 3 Using Adverbs

Provide adverbs to modify these verbs, using a dictionary, a thesaurus, or the resources designated by your instructor. Use only single words, not adverb phrases.

1. Write _____ and clearly.

2. Run _____ and get help.

3. Talk _____ and carry a big stick.

4. Walk _____ and think fast.

5. Marry _____ and suffer at leisure.

6. Smile _____ at your boss.

7. Drive _____ and carefully.

8. Leave _____ and forget my name.

9. Laugh _____ at adversity.

10. Study _____ and get smart.

∿ Comparative and Superlative Forms

For making comparisons, most adjectives and adverbs have three different forms: the positive (one), the comparative (two), and the superlative (three or more).

Adjectives

1. Some adjectives follow a regular pattern:

Positive (one)	Comparative (two)	Superlative (three or more)
nice	nicer	nicest
rich	richer	richest
big	bigger	biggest
tall	taller	tallest
lonely	lonelier	loneliest
terrible	more terrible	most terrible
beautiful	more beautiful	most beautiful

These are usually the rules:

a. Add -er to short adjectives (one or two syllbles) to rank units of two:

Julian is *nicer* than Sam.

b. Add -est to short adjectives (one or two syllbles) to rank units of three or more:

Of the fifty people I know, Julian is the *kindest*.

c. Add the word *more* to long adjectives (three or more syllbles) to rank units of two.

My hometown is *more beautiful* than yours.

d. Add the word *most* to long adjectives (three or more syllbles) to rank units of three or more.

My hometown is the *most beautiful* in all America.

2. Some adjectives are irregular in the way they change to show comparison.

Positive (one)	Comparative (two)	Superlative (three or more)
good	better	best
bad	worse	worst

Adverbs

1. For most adverbs, use the word *more* before the comparative form (two) and the word *most* before the superlative form (three or more).

> Pedro performed *skillfully*. (modifier)
>
> Pedro performed *more skillfully* than Kari. (comparative modifier)
>
> But Lorena performed *most skillfully* of all. (superlative modifier)

2. Avoid double negatives. Words such as *no, not, none, nothing, never, hardly, barely,* and *scarcely* should not be combined.

> DOUBLE NEGATIVE   I do *not* have *no* time for recreation. (incorrect)
>
> SINGLE NEGATIVE   I have *no* time for recreation. (correct)
>
> DOUBLE NEGATIVE   I've *hardly never* lied. (incorrect)
>
> SINGLE NEGATIVE   I've *hardly* ever lied. (correct)

3. Do not confuse adjectives with adverbs. Among the most commonly confused adjectives and adverbs are *good/well, bad/badly,* and *real/really.* The words *good, bad,* and *real* are always adjectives. *Well* is sometimes an adjective. The words *badly* and *really* are always adverbs. *Well* is usually an adverb.

   To distinguish these words, consider what is being modified. Remember that adjectives modify nouns and pronouns and that adverbs modify verbs, adjectives, and other adverbs.

> WRONG   I feel *badly* today. (We're concerned with the condition of *I*.)
>
> RIGHT   I feel *bad* today. (The adjective *bad* modifies the pronoun *I*.)
>
> WRONG   She feels *well* about that choice. (We're concerned with the condition of *she*, a pronoun, not the quality of *feels*, a verb.)

RIGHT   She feels *good* about that choice. (The adjective *good* modifies the pronoun *she*.)

WRONG   Wyatt plays the piano *good*. (The adjective *good* modifies the verb *plays*, but adjectives should not modify verbs.)

RIGHT   Wyatt plays the piano *well*. (The adverb *well* modifies the verb *plays*.)

WRONG   He did *real* well. (Here the adjective *real* modifies the adverb *well*, but adjectives should not modify adverbs.)

RIGHT   He did *really* well. (The adverb *really* modifies the adverb *well*.)

4. Do not use an adverb such as *very*, *more*, or *most* before absolute adjectives such as *perfect*, *round*, *unique*, *square*, and *straight*.

WRONG   It is more round. (Nothing can be rounder than round).

RIGHT   It is round.

RIGHT   It is more nearly round.

Exercise 4   Selecting Adjectives and Adverbs

Underline the correct word or words.

1. Betty Skelton was one of the (most, more) successful female stunt pilots of the 1940s and 1950s.

2. In the 1930s and 1940s, the public was (real, really) interested in watching acrobatic air shows.

3. Skelton was (not hardly, hardly) going to sit there and watch the men have all the fun.

4. She wanted (bad, badly) to learn to fly, and she was (real, really) adventurous, so she learned to perform daredevil feats.

5. Her small, agile airplane, which was named Little Stinker, performed tricks (well, good).

6. One of her (better, best) stunts was the inverted ribbon cut.

7. It was a (real, really) thrill to watch her fly upside down twelve feet off the ground and use her propeller to slice a foil strip strung between two poles.

8. The crowd could (not hardly, hardly) contain its excitement.

9. She earned only $25 for each air show, so the pay was (bad, badly).

10. But according to Betty, her six-year acrobatic flying career was the (more, most) fun time in her life.

Exercise 5 Selecting Adjectives and Adverbs

Correct any problems with adjectives and adverbs in the following sentences.

1. In the beginning, back in 1173, the people of Pisa wanted their new *campanille*, or bell tower, to be the most perfect one ever built.

2. The Tower of Pisa was built over near two centuries and involved the design of several architects.

3. Today the "Leaning Tower of Pisa" is recognized as one of the more beautiful buildings in the world, and one of the strangest.

4. The foundation was not dug deep enough in the unstable soil, so one side of the tower has sunk lower than the other, giving the tower its distinctive lean.

5. The first story of the tower is decorated with real nice classical columns and capitals.

6. The next six stories are done in the Romanesque style, and they look really well.

7. The top story contains the more beautiful sounding bells in all of Pisa.

8. Most Italians feel badly about the precarious state of the tower, and numerous attempts have been made to correct or stop the increase in its degree of lean.

9. Mussolini ordered the foundation filled with cement, but that made the problem worst.

10. An international task force of engineers, scientists, and historians worked together for ten years to help stop the further lean of the building, and since 2001 there has been no danger of the building falling no more.

Exercise 6   Selecting Adjectives and Adverbs

Cross out the mistake in each sentence and write in the correction above it.

1. Vincent van Gogh is one of the better known painters in the world.

2. He is recognized for his real unique use of color and subject material.

3. It would be difficult to create anything more perfect than his masterpiece, "Café Terrace at Night."

4. Van Gogh painted real good, and his work influenced other painters such as Matisse, Kandinsky, and Nolde.

5. One of his beautifullest paintings is titled "Starry Night" and features a brilliant depiction of the night sky.

6. Born in 1853, van Gogh only lived until 1890, but he produced some of the better paintings of the post-Impressionist school.

7. Early in life, he had religious training, but his later years in boarding went bad, so he dropped out.

8. After dropping out of school, he felt well about working for an art dealer.

9. Van Gogh's work took him from the Netherlands to London, and eventually France, a country with some of the more beautiful countrysides and cities in the world.

10. The young man was not real successful as he tried many odd jobs, even attempting to be a village preacher at one point.

11. At age 27, van Gogh finally became a painter, thereby ensuring himself of posthumously fame and a lifetime of poverty.

12. Along with mental illness—most likely paranoid schizophrenia—van Gogh had the more unfortunate habit of

drinking a powerful alcoholic beverage popular at the time, absinthe.

13. Van Gogh often felt badly and would try to think more clear by drinking alcohol.

14. The poorly artist had a few relationships with women that ended badly.

15. For instance, he lived with a prostitute and her two children for about two years, but she could not stand no more of his problems and left.

16. Now living in France, van Gogh, started to do some of his better paintings.

17. In 1888, van Gogh, in a real infamous episode, cut off part of his ear and gave it to a prostitute, telling her that it was a "precious" gift.

18. The artist obviously had emotionally troubles and was sent to an asylum to recuperate.

19. After his release, he continued to paint masterpieces that, unbelievably, hardly no one wanted to buy.

20. In 1890, van Gogh tragically shot himself in the chest, never knowing that he would eventually be regarded as one of the most great painters of all time.

⌒ Dangling and Misplaced Modifiers

Modifiers should clearly relate to the word or words they modify.

1. A modifier that gives information but doesn't refer to a word or group of words already in the sentence is called a **dangling modifier**.

DANGLING	*Walking down the street,* a snake startled him. (The modifier is not connected grammatically to a particular word.)
CORRECT	*Walking down the street,* Don was startled by a snake.
CORRECT	As *Don* walked down the street, *he* was startled by a snake.
DANGLING	*At the age of six,* my uncle died. (Who was six years old? The person isn't mentioned in the modifier.)
CORRECT	*When I was six,* my uncle died.

2. A modifier that is placed so that it modifies the wrong word or words is called a **misplaced modifier**. The term also applies to words that are positioned to unnecessarily divide closely related parts of sentences such as infinitives (*to* plus verb) or subjects and verbs.

MISPLACED	The sick man went to a doctor *with a high fever.*
CORRECT	The sick man *with a high fever* went to a doctor.
MISPLACED	I saw a great movie *sitting in my pickup.*
CORRECT	*Sitting in my pickup,* I saw a great movie.
MISPLACED	Kim found many new graves *walking through the cemetery.*
CORRECT	*Walking through the cemetery,* Kim found many new graves.
MISPLACED	I forgot all about my sick dog *kissing my girlfriend.*
CORRECT	*Kissing my girlfriend,* I forgot all about my sick dog.
MISPLACED	They tried to *earnestly and sincerely* complete the task. (splitting of the infinitive *to complete*)
CORRECT	They tried *earnestly and sincerely* to complete the task.

MISPLACED   My neighbor, *while walking to the store,* was mugged. (unnecessarily dividing the subject and verb)

CORRECT   *While walking to the store,* my neighbor was mugged.

Try this procedure in working with the following exercises.

1. Circle the modifier.
2. Draw an arrow from the modifier to the word or words it modifies.
3. If the modifier does not relate directly to anything in the sentence, it is dangling, and you must recast the sentence.
4. If the modifier does not modify the nearest word or words, or if it interrupts related sentence parts, it is misplaced and you need to reposition it.

Exercise 7   Correcting Dangling and Misplaced Modifiers

Circle the dangling (D) or misplaced (M) modifier in each of the following sentences. Identify the type of modifier by writing D or M in the blank to the left. Rewrite each sentence in the space provided.

_____   1. Driving through the Brazilian rain forest, leaf-cutter ants were spotted going about their work.

_____

_____   2. This tribe of ants is one of the few creatures on this planet that grows food.

_____

_____   3. Leaf-cutter ants learned to cleverly farm more than 50 million years ago.

_____

_____   4. Climbing trees, the leaves are cut down and bitten into the shape of half-moons.

_____

_____   5. Then each ant hoists a leaf and carries it back down the tree toward the nest, weighing ten times more than it does.

_____   6. Marching home with their leaves, a parade of fluttering green flags is what the ants resemble.

_____   7. Carried into the subterranean tunnels of the nest, the leaf-cutters deposit their cargo.

_____   8. Taking over, the leaves are cleaned, clipped, and spread with secretions from tiny gardener ants' bodies.

_____   9. Lined up in neat rows, the ants place fungus on the hunks of leaves.

_____   10. Cultivated for food, the ants use the leaves as fertilizer for their fungus garden.

Exercise 8   Correcting Dangling and Misplaced Modifiers

Circle the dangling (D) or misplaced (M) modifier in each of the following sentences. Identify the type of modifier by writing D or M in the blank to the left. Rewrite each sentence in the space provided.

_____   1. I observed the parade of floats and marching bands on the rooftop.

_____   2. Having no money, my piano had to be pawned for cash.

_____

_____   3. The alleged burglar addressed the judge on his knees.

_____

_____   4. Freshly snared from the ocean floor, he enjoyed the delicious lobster.

_____

_____   5. Wearing a strapless velvet evening gown, Bob thought his wife looked ravishing.

_____

_____   6. The student asked to see the school nurse with a sore throat.

_____

_____   7. The lost child held on tight to the detective crying for his mommy.

_____

_____   8. Cursing like a longshoreman, the baby finally arrived after her thirty-sixth hour of labor.

_____

_____   9. By jumping on a trampoline, your heart gets a good cardiovascular workout.

_____

_____   10. The outlaw phoned his granny in a pickle.

_____

◜◞ Chapter Review

Exercise 9 Writing Sentences with Adjectives and Adverbs

Write a sentence using each of the following words.

1. good, better, best _____

    _____

    _____

2. good, well _____

    _____

3. more, most _____

    _____

4. bad, badly _____

    _____

5. real, really _____

    _____

10

Punctuation and
Capitalization

Understanding punctuation will help you write better. If you aren't sure how to punctuate a compound or a compound-complex sentence, then you probably will not write one. If you don't know how to show that some of your words come from other sources, you may mislead your reader. And if you misuse punctuation, you will force your readers to struggle to get your message. So take the time to review and master the mechanics. Your efforts will be rewarded.

End Punctuation

Periods

1. Place a period after a statement.

   The weather is beautiful today.

2. Place a period after common abbreviations.

   Dr.   Mr.   Mrs.   Dec.   a.m.

   EXCEPTIONS: FBI   UN   NAACP   FHA   NATO

3. Use an ellipsis—three periods within a sentence and four periods at the end of a sentence—to indicate that words have been omitted from quoted material.

   He stopped walking and the buildings . . . rose up out of the misty courtroom. . . . (James Thurber, "The Secret Life of Walter Mitty")

Question Marks

1. Place a question mark at the end of a direct question.

   Will you go to the country tomorrow?

152

2. Use a single question mark in sentence constructions that contain a double question—that is, a quoted question within a question.

   Mr. Martin said, "Did he say, 'Are you going?'"

3. Do *not* use a question mark after an indirect (reported) question.

   She asked me what caused the slide.

Exclamation Points

1. Place an exclamation point after a word or a group of words that expresses strong feeling.

   Oh!   What a night!   Help!   You've got to be kidding!

2. Do not overwork the exclamation point. Do not use double exclamation points. Use the period or comma for mild exclamatory words, phrases, or sentences.

   Oh, we can leave now.

〜 Commas

Commas to Separate

1. Use a comma to separate main clauses joined by one of the coordinating conjunctions commonly referred to by the acronym FANBOYS: *for*, *and*, *nor*, *but*, *or*, *yet*, *so*. The comma may be omitted if the clauses are brief and parallel.

   We traveled many miles to see the game, *but* it was canceled.
   Adriana left and I remained. (brief and parallel clauses)

2. Use a comma after introductory dependent clauses and long introductory phrases (generally, four or more words is considered long).

   Before the arrival of the shipment, the boss had written a letter protesting the delay. (two prepositional phrases)
   If you don't hear from me, assume that I am lost. (introductory clause, an adverbial modifier)
   In winter we skate on the river. (short modifier, no comma)

3. Use a comma to separate words, phrases, and clauses in a series.

   Red, *white*, and *blue* were her favorite colors. (words)

Ed drove *down the street, onto the freeway,* and *into the state of Texas.* (phrases)

When the television was off, when the children were in bed, and when the dog was asleep, Mother could work on her research paper. (clauses)

4. Do *not* use a comma when coordinating conjunctions connect all the elements in a series.

   He bought apples *and* pears *and* grapes.

5. Use a comma to separate coordinate adjectives that are not joined by *and* that modify the same noun.

   I need a *sturdy, reliable* truck.

6. Use a comma to separate adjectives that are coordinate. Try this technique to determine whether the adjectives are coordinate: Put *and* between the adjectives. If it fits naturally, the adjectives are coordinate and require a comma; if it does not, they are not coordinate, and you do not need a comma.

   Wanda is a kind, beautiful person. (kind *and* beautiful—natural, hence the comma)

   I built a red brick wall. (red *and* brick wall—not natural, no comma)

7. Use a comma to separate sentence elements that might be misread.

   Inside the dog scratched his fleas.

   Inside, the dog scratched his fleas.

   Without benefit of the comma, the reader might initially misunderstand the relationship among the first three words.

Commas to Set Off

1. Use commas to set off (enclose) adjectives in pairs that follow a noun.

   The scouts, *tired and hungry,* marched back to camp.

2. Use commas to set off nonessential (unnecessary for meaning of the sentence) words, phrases, and clauses.

   My brother, *a student at Ohio University,* is visiting me. (If you drop the phrase, the basic meaning of the sentence remains intact.)

Marla, *who studied hard*, will pass. (The clause is not essential to the basic meaning of the sentence.)

All students *who studied hard* will pass. (Here the clause *is* essential. If you remove it, you would have *All students will pass*, which is not necessarily true.)

I shall not stop searching *until I find the treasure*. (A dependent clause at the end of a sentence is usually not set off with a comma. However, a clause beginning with the word *though, although*, or *whereas* will be set off regardless of where it is located.)

I felt unsatisfied, *though we had won the game*. (The clause begins with *though*.)

3. Use commas to set off parenthetical elements such as mild interjections (*oh, well, yes, no*, and others), most conjunctive adverbs (*however, otherwise, therefore, similarly, hence, on the one hand, on the other hand*, and *consequently*, but not *then, thus, soon, now*, and *also*), quotation indicators, and special abbreviations (*etc., i.e., e.g.*, and others).

Oh, what a silly question! (mild interjection)

It is necessary, *of course*, to leave now. (sentence modifier)

We left early; *however*, we missed the train anyway. (conjunctive adverb)

"When I was in school," *he said*, "I read widely." (quotation indicators)

Books, papers, pens, *etc.*, were scattered on the floor. (The abbreviation *etc.*, however, should be used sparingly.)

4. Use commas to set off nouns used as direct address.

Play it again, *Sam*.

Please tell us the answer, *Rashan*, so we can discuss it.

5. Use commas to separate the numbers in a date.

August *19, 1961*, is a day I will remember.

6. Do not use commas if the day of the month is not specified or if the day is given before the month.

June is my favorite month.

Another day I will never forget is 4 June 1965.

7. Use commas to separate the city from the state. No comma is used between the state and the zip code.

Walnut, CA 91789

8. Use a comma following the salutation of a friendly letter and the complimentary closing in any letter.

Dear John,
Sincerely,

9. Use a comma in numbers to set off groups of three digits. However, omit the comma in dates, serial numbers, page numbers, years, and street numbers.

The total assets were $2,000,000.
I look forward to the year 2025.

Exercise 1   Using Commas

Insert commas where needed.

1. In *Frankenstein* the original classic horror thriller written by Mary Shelley and published on October 3 1818 Victor Frankenstein was a gifted dedicated student.

2. While he studied science at the university he came upon the secret of how to create life.

3. Being more interested in simple practical matters than in theory he set out to construct a living breathing creature.

4. Victor who was very much concerned about process first needed to gather the materials necessary for his experiment.

5. He went all around town picking up body parts and he stored them in his laboratory.

6. The dissecting room at a local hospital provided him with the most basic articles and he was very grateful.

7. Local butcher shops had plenty of items perhaps including some spare ribs.

8. Finally he was ready to begin construction of a strange humanlike creature.

9. He made a creature that was eight feet tall four feet wide and very strong.

10. The face of the creature which could be described only as hideous was not easy to look upon.

11. One night while Victor was sleeping lightly the monster lonely and troubled came to his bedroom.

12. Victor screamed loudly and the monster ran away in disappointment.

13. Victor developed brain fever which was a result of the encounter.

14. When Victor recovered from his illness he discovered that one of his brothers had been murdered by an unknown person.

15. In despair and befuddlement Victor went to a remote wilderness to sort out his problems.

16. One day when he was out walking Victor saw a strange lumbering creature running into the mountains.

17. Victor chased the creature but he was unable to catch it.

18. Soon after he sat down to rest and the creature appeared before him.

19. It was Victor Frankenstein's monster who had come to talk to him.

20. With a great deal of self-pity the monster explained that he was very sad because people were unkind to him.

Exercise 2 Using Commas

Insert commas where needed.

1. Frankenstein's monster distraught and desperate told a story of acute loneliness.

2. After leaving Victor Frankenstein's house he had gone to live in the country.

3. He had tried diligently to help the simple gentle people by bringing them firewood.

4. They took the firewood; however they were at first frightened and then angry.

5. The monster very upset and dejected had gone back to the city.

6. There he killed Victor's innocent unsuspecting brother and he then cleverly tried to place the blame on someone else.

7. Listening to the monster in horror Victor Frankenstein realized what he had done in this act of creation.

8. The monster started making demands and it was clear that he would force Victor to carry them out.

9. He said that if Victor did not make a suitable female companion for him he would begin killing human beings at random.

10. Victor went away gathered up some more parts and started building a bride for the monster.

11. The monster waited in eager anticipation but he was to be sorely disappointed.

12. Victor became disgusted with his project and he destroyed all the tissue just before it came to life.

13. Needless to say the monster was deeply distressed by this unexpected shocking development.

14. Before the monster ran away he swore to get revenge on Victor's wedding night.

15. When Victor got married he armed himself fully for he expected a visit from the enraged vengeful monster.

16. On the night of the wedding the monster slipped into the bridal chambers and strangled the horrified unlucky bride.

17. Victor himself vowed to avenge the murder by killing the monster but the monster was nowhere to be found.

18. Victor finally died in a cabin in the desolate frozen lands of the North and much later his body was found by a friend.

19. The monster dropped by for one last visit for he wanted to complain about his unhappy life.

20. He said that Victor had created a man without a friend love or
    even a soul and therefore Victor was more wicked than anyone.

⌒ Semicolons

The semicolon indicates a stronger division than the comma. It is
used principally to separate independent clauses within a sentence.

1. Use a semicolon to separate independent clauses not joined by a
   coordinating conjunction.

   You must buy that car today; tomorrow will be too late.

2. Use a semicolon between two independent clauses joined by a
   conjunctive adverb such as one of the HOTSHOT CAT words
   (*however, otherwise, therefore, similarly, hence, on the other
   hand, then, consequently, accordingly, thus*).

   It was very late; therefore, I remained at the hotel.

3. Use a semicolon to separate main clauses joined by a coordinating conjunction if one or both of these clauses contain possibly
   distracting commas.

   Byron, the famous English poet, was buried in Greece; and Shelley, who was his friend and fellow poet, was buried in Italy.

4. Use a semicolon in a series between items that themselves contain commas.

   Lee has lived in Glendora, California; Fort Worth, Texas; Tribbey,
   Oklahoma; and Gulfport, Mississippi.

Exercise 3   Using Semicolons and Commas

Insert semicolons and commas where needed.

1. Once upon a time, there was a young woman named Cyberella
   she lived in Oklahoma with an evil stepmother and an
   obnoxious stepsister.

2. One night at eleven her wretched stepfamily was snoring raucously and Cyberella was busily dusting the family computer which someone had left running.

3. It was then that Cyberella inadvertently hit the Instant Internet button therefore the screen lit up.

4. She had never been permitted to use the Internet but she had enviously watched her evil stepfamily at the keyboard.

5. Cyberella created the screen name Cool4aday and logged on for fun and education naturally she started with the index of chat rooms.

6. She was delighted with her unexpected opportunity however she realized that the computer was programmed to go out of commission at midnight.

7. Now she was a free-spirited cyberspace explorer surfing the World Wide Web at midnight she would turn back into a servant ripping out cobwebs and capturing dust bunnies.

8. Cyberella spotted a chat room called "Talk to the Prince" feeling like a princess she joined in the conversation.

9. To her amazement she discovered that she was chatting with a real prince Prince Igor of Transylvania in fact he seemed to like her.

10. Prince Igor boldly invited Cyberella to accompany him to a private chat room breathlessly she said yes and followed him with demure keystrokes.

11. They chatted shyly and then passionately for almost an hour and soon the prince became royally enamored by the way she processed thought noticing that she wrote skillfully using her spell checker and grammar checker in a most delicate way.

12. Cyberella wanted to tell Prince Igor explicitly what was in her heart therefore she often used the computer thesaurus feature impressing him further with her highly eloquent diction.

13. Prince Igor was about to ask the royal marriage question then Cyberella heard the clock strike her computer went dark and she believed she would never again chat with her sweet prince.

14. Prince Igor was devastated and vowed to find this lovely correspondent he therefore directed his army to undertake a royal search that would properly but legally identify Cool4aday and expose all impostors.

15. The soldiers would test the computer-assisted writing skills of everyone in the world if necessary moreover they would even provide laptops for any computerless woman who looked as if she could possibly be the mystery writer.

16. Cyberella had informed Prince Igor that she was from the American Southwest a fact that enabled him to focus his search.

17. Following electronic clues, the soldiers visited Amarillo Texas Tucumcari New Mexico Tulsa Oklahoma and Window Rock Arizona.

18. At last a soldier came to Cyberella's house and was greeted by the obnoxious stepsister who claimed that she was Cool4aday and began to chat online with Prince Igor however the stepsister forgot to use her spell checker and the prince flamed a rejection.

19. Then the soldier handed Cyberella a laptop computer and instructions of course both the wicked stepmother and the obnoxious stepsister scoffed.

20. Nevertheless, Cyberella was verified as Cool4aday and the prince was wildly elated therefore he declared an international holiday slapped his leg with glee and offered to grant her fondest wish.

21. "Does that mean I get this laptop for myself?" Cyberella asked and Prince Igor a bit humbled by her response said "No that means you get me for yourself."

22. "Oh, that's very very nice but may I also have this laptop?" Cyberella asked striking a hard bargain as she fondly hugged the computer.

23. "Yes" Prince Igor said. "I'll even toss in a laser printer and I'll
    add a few pounds of copy paper and a stack of dungeon-and-
    dragon software customized in one of my own castles."

24. They got married and lived happily ever after for a while then
    the wicked stepfamily tried to move into the palace but they
    were arrested and were no longer allowed to use the Internet in
    Transylvania or Oklahoma until they had passed a writing test
    which they never did.

⌒ Quotation Marks

Quotation marks are used principally to set off direct quotations.
A direct quotation consists of material taken from the written work
or the direct speech of others; it is set off by double quotation marks.
Single quotation marks are used to set off a quotation within a
quotation.

> DOUBLE QUOTATION MARKS   He said, "I don't remember."
>
> SINGLE QUOTATION MARKS   He said, "I don't remember if she
> said, 'Wait for me.'"

1. Use double quotation marks to set off direct quotations.

   Jorell said, "Give me the book."

   As Edward McNeil writes of the Greek achievement: "To an extent never before realized, mind was supreme over faith."

2. Use double quotation marks to set off titles of shorter pieces of
   writing, such as magazine articles, essays, short stories, short
   poems, one-act plays, chapters in books, songs, and separate
   pieces of writing published as part of a larger work.

   The book *Literature: Structure, Sound, and Sense* contains a
   deeply moving poem titled "On Wenlock Edge."

Have you read "The Use of Force," a short story by William Carlos Williams?

My favorite Elvis song is "Don't Be Cruel."

3. Use double quotation marks to set off slang, technical terms, and special words.

   There are many aristocrats, but Elvis is the only true "King." (special word)

   The "platoon system" changed the game of football. (technical term)

4. Use double quotation marks in writing dialogue (conversation). Write each speech unit as a separate paragraph and set it off with double quotation marks.

   "Will you go with me?" Cole asked.

   "Yes," Nikita replied. "Are you ready now?"

5. Use single quotation marks to set off a quotation within a quotation.

   Professor Baxter said, "You should remember Shakespeare's words 'All the world's a stage.'"

6. Do *not* use quotation marks for indirect quotations.

   WRONG   He said that "he would bring the supplies."

   RIGHT   He said that he would bring the supplies.

7. Do *not* use quotation marks for the title on your own written work. If you refer to that title in another piece of writing, however, you need the quotation marks.

Punctuation with Quotation Marks

1. A period or comma is always placed *inside* the quotation marks.

   Our assignment for Monday was to read Poe's poem "The Raven."

   "I will read you the story," he said. "It's a good one."

2. A semicolon or colon is always placed *outside* the quotation marks.

   He read Robert Frost's poem "Design"; then he gave the examination.

3. A question mark, an exclamation point, or a dash is placed *out-side* the quotation marks when it applies to the entire sentence and *inside* the quotation marks when it applies to the material in quotation marks.

> He asked, "Am I responsible for everything?" (quoted question within a statement)
>
> Did you hear him say, "I have the answer"? (statement within a question)
>
> Did she say, "Are you ready?" (question within a question)
>
> She shouted, "Impossible!" (exclamation)
>
> "I hope—that is, I—" he began. (dash)

⌐✓ Italics

Italic print (slanting type) is used to call special attention to certain words or groups of words. In handwriting, such words are underlined.

1. Italicize (underline) foreign words and phrases that are still listed in the dictionary as foreign.

> *c'est la vie*   *Weltschmerz*

2. Italicize (underline) titles of books (except the Bible); long poems; plays; magazines; motion pictures; musical compositions; newspapers; works of art; names of aircraft; names of ships; and letters, figures, and words.

> I think Hemingway's best novel is *A Farewell to Arms.*
>
> His source material was taken from *Time, Newsweek,* and the Los Angeles *Times.* (Sometimes the name of the city in titles of newspapers is italicized—for example, the *New York Times.*)
>
> The *Mona Lisa* is my favorite painting.

3. Italicize (underline) the names of ships, airplanes, spacecraft, and trains.

> *Queen Mary*   *Lurline*   *Stockholm*
>
> *Challenger*   *Voyager 2*

4. Italicize (underline) to distinguish letters, figures, and words when they refer to themselves rather than to the ideas or things they usually represent.

Do not leave the *o* out of *sophomore*.
Your *3*'s look like *5*'s.

Exercise 4   Using Quotation Marks and Italics

Insert quotation marks and italics (underlining) as needed.

1. Professor Jones said, Now we will read from The Complete Works of Edgar Allan Poe.

2. The enthusiastic students shouted, We like Poe! We like Poe!

3. The professor lectured for fifty-seven minutes before he finally said, In conclusion, Poe was an unappreciated writer during his lifetime.

4. The next speaker said, I believe that Poe said, A short story should be short enough so that a person can read it in one sitting.

5. Then, while students squirmed, he read The Fall of the House of Usher in sixty-eight minutes.

6. Now we will do some reading in unison, said Professor Jones.

7. The students were not pleased that they would be reading only the word Nevermore from the poem The Raven.

8. The professor reached into his bag of props, took out a dark, feathered object, and said, I have brought a stuffed raven.

9. That's not a raven. That's a crow, said a student who was

   majoring in ornithology.

10. The professor waggled his finger playfully at his audience and

    said, I believe Coleridge once observed, Art sometimes requires

    the willing suspension of disbelief.

〰 Dashes

The dash is used when a stronger break than the comma is needed. The dash is typed as two hyphens with no space before or after them (--).

1. Use a dash to indicate a sudden change in sentence construction or an abrupt break in thought.

   Here is the true reason—but maybe you don't care.

2. Use a dash after an introductory list. The words *these, those, all,* and occasionally *such* introduce the summarizing statement.

   English, French, history—these are the subjects I like.

   Dodgers, Giants, Yankees—such names bring back memories of exciting World Series games.

3. Use a dash to set off material that interrupts the flow of an idea, sets off material for emphasis, or restates an idea as an appositive.

   You are—I am certain—not serious. (interrupting)

   Our next question is—how much money did we raise? (emphasis)

   Dione plays the kazoo—an instrument with a buzz. (restatement)

4. Use a dash to indicate an unfinished statement, an omitted word, or an interruption. Such interruptions usually occur in dialogue.

   Susan said, "Shall we—" (no period)

   "I only wanted—" Jason remarked. (no comma)

5. Do *not* use a dash in places in which other marks of punctuation would be more appropriate.

> WRONG   Lupe found the store—and she shopped.
> RIGHT   Lupe found the store, and she shopped.
> WRONG   I think it is too early to go—
> RIGHT   I think it is too early to go.

∾ Colons

The colon is a formal mark of punctuation used chiefly to introduce something that is to follow, such as a list, a quotation, or an explanation.

1. Use a colon after a main clause to introduce a formal list, an emphatic or a long restatement (appositive), an explanation, an emphatic statement, or a summary.

> These cars are my favorites: Cadillac, Chevrolet, Buick, Honda, and Toyota. (list)
>
> He worked toward one objective: a degree. (restatement or appositive)
>
> Let me emphasize one point: I do not accept late papers. (emphatic statement)

2. Use a colon to introduce a formal quotation or a formal question.

> Shakespeare's Polonius said: "Neither a borrower nor a lender be." (formal quotation)
>
> The question is this: Shall we surrender? (formal question)

3. Use a colon in the following conventional ways: to separate a title and subtitle, a chapter and verse in the Bible, and hours and minutes; and after the salutation in a formal business letter.

> TITLE AND SUBTITLE   *Korea: A Country Divided*
> CHAPTER AND VERSE   Genesis 4:12
> HOUR AND MINUTES   8:25 p.m.
> SALUTATION   Dear Ms. Johnson:

〰 Parentheses

1. Parentheses are used to set off material that is not part of the main sentence but is too important to omit altogether. In this category are numbers that designate items in a series, amplifying references, explanations, directions, and qualifications.

   > He offered two reasons for his losing: (1) he was tired; (2) he was out of condition. (numbers)

   > Review the chapters on the Civil War (6, 7, and 8) for the next class meeting. (references)

   > Her husband (she had been married about a year) died last week. (explanation)

2. Use a comma, semicolon, and colon after the parentheses when the sentence punctuation requires their use.

   > Although I have not lived here long (I arrived in 2002), this place feels like my only true home.

   Use a period, a question mark, and an exclamation point in appropriate positions, depending on whether they go with the material within the parentheses or with the entire sentence.

   > The greatest English poet of the seventeenth century was John Milton (1608–1674).

   > The greatest English poet of the seventeenth century was John Milton. (Some might not agree; I myself favor Andrew Marvell.)

〰 Brackets

Brackets are used within a quotation to set off editorial additions or corrections made by the person who is quoting.

> Churchill said: "It [the Yalta agreement] contained many mistakes."

〰 Apostrophes

The apostrophe is used with nouns and indefinite pronouns to show possession; to show the omission of letters and figures in contractions; and to form the plurals of letters, figures, and words referred to as words.

1. A possessive shows that something is owned by someone. Use an apostrophe and -*s* to form the possessive of a noun, singular or plural, that does not end in -*s*.

   man's coat   women's suits

2. Use an apostrophe alone to form the possessive of a plural noun ending in -*s*.

   girls' clothes   the Browns' house

3. Use an apostrophe and -*s* or the apostrophe alone to form the possessive of singular nouns ending in -*s*. Use the apostrophe and -*s* only when you would pronounce the *s*.

   James' hat *or* (if you would pronounce the *s*) James's hat

4. Use an apostrophe and -*s* to form the possessive of certain indefinite pronouns.

   everybody's idea   one's meat   another's poison

5. Use an apostrophe to indicate that letters or figures have been omitted.

   o'clock (short for *of the clock*)   in the '80s (short for *1980s*)

6. Use an apostrophe to indicate the plural of letters, figures, and words used as words.

   Dot your *i*'s.   five *8*'s   *and*'s

7. Use an apostrophe with pronouns only when you are making a contraction. A contraction is a combination of two words. The apostrophe in a contraction indicates where a letter has been omitted.

   it is = it's

   she has = she's

   you are = you're

If no letters have been left out, don't use an apostrophe.

   WRONG   The dog bit it's tail. (not a contraction)
   RIGHT   The dog bit its tail.

WRONG   Whose the leader now?

RIGHT   Who's the leader now? (a contraction of *who is*)

WRONG   Its a big problem.

RIGHT   It's a big problem. (a contraction of *it is*)

⌒ Hyphens

The hyphen brings two or more words together into a single compound word. Correct hyphenation, therefore, is essentially a spelling problem rather than one of punctuation. Because the hyphen is not used with any degree of consistency, consult your dictionary for current usage. Study the following as a beginning guide.

1. Use a hyphen to separate the parts of many compound words.

   brother-in-law   go-between

2. Use a hyphen between prefixes and suffixes and proper names.

   all-American   mid-Atlantic

3. Use a hyphen to join two or more words used as a single adjective modifier before a noun.

   bluish-gray eyes   first-class service

4. Use a hyphen with spelled-out compound numbers through ninety-nine, and with fractions.

   twenty-six   two-thirds

Note: Dates, street addresses, numbers requiring more than two words, chapter and page numbers, time followed directly by *a.m.* or *p.m.*, and figures after a dollar sign or before measurement abbreviations are usually written as figures, not words.

⌒ Capitalization

In English, there are many conventions concerning the use of capital letters. Here are some of them.

1. Capitalize the first word of a sentence.

2. Capitalize proper nouns and adjectives derived from proper nouns.

Names of persons
Edward Jones

Adjectives derived from proper nouns
a Shakespearean sonnet   a Miltonic sonnet

Countries, nationalities, races, languages
Germany   English   Spanish   Chinese

States, regions, localities, other geographical divisions
California   the Far East   the South

Oceans, lakes, mountains, deserts, streets, parks
Lake Superior   Fifth Avenue   Sahara Desert

Educational institutions, schools, courses
Santa Ana College   Spanish 3   Joe Hill School
Rowland High School

Organizations and their members
Boston Red Sox   Boy Scouts   Audubon Society

Corporations, governmental agencies or departments, trade names
U.S. Steel Corporation   Treasury Department
White Memorial Library   Coke

Calendar references such as holidays, days of the week, months
Easter   Tuesday   January

Historic eras, periods, documents, laws
Declaration of Independence   Geneva Convention
First Crusade   Romantic Age

3. Capitalize words denoting family relationships when they are used before a name or substituted for a name.

Rex walked with his nephew and Aunt Grace.

but

Rex walked with his nephew and his aunt.

Grandmother and Mother are away on vacation.

but

My grandmother and my mother are away on vacation.

4. Capitalize abbreviations after names.

Henry White Jr.

Juan Gomez, M.D.

5. Capitalize titles of themes, books, plays, movies, poems, magazines, newspapers, musical compositions, songs, and works of

art. Do not capitalize short conjunctions and prepositions unless they come at the beginning or the end of the title.

Desire Under the Elms   *Terminator*
Last of the Mohicans   *Of Mice and Men*
"Blueberry Hill"

6. Capitalize any title preceding a name or used as a substitute for a name. Do not capitalize a title following a name.

Judge Wong   Alfred Wong, a judge
General Clark   Raymond Clark, a general
Professor Fuentes   Harry Jones, the former president

Exercise 5   Using Capital Letters and All Punctuation Marks

Correct capitalization and insert punctuation marks as needed.

will rogers 1879–1935 was a famous movie star newspaper

writer and lecturer. A part cherokee indian he was born in what

was then indian territory before oklahoma became a state. He is es-

pecially known for his humor and his social and political criticism.

He said my ancestors may not have come over on the *mayflower,*

but they met em at the boat. He said that when many oklahomans

moved to california in the early 1930s the average IQ increased

in both states. In his early years, he was a first class performer in

rodeos circuses and variety shows. When he performed in variety

shows he often twirled a rope. He usually began his presentations

by saying all I know is what I read in the papers. Continuing to be

close to his oklahoma roots he appeared in fifty one silent movies and twenty one talking movies. At the age of fifty six he was killed in an airplane crash near Point Barrow Alaska. He was so popular and influential that his statue now stands in washington d.c. On another statue of him in Claremore Oklahoma is inscribed one of his most famous sayings I never met a man I didn't like.

Exercise 6 Using Capital Letters and All Punctuation Marks
Correct capitalization and insert punctuation marks as needed.

Jack (Jackie) Roosevelt Robinson 1919–1972 was born in Pasadena California. After excelling in sports in high school and community college he transferred to UCLA, where he lettered in four sports baseball, basketball, football, and track. In world war II he was commissioned second lieutenant in the army. After he was discharged he joined the negro league as a player with the Kansas City Monarchs for $100 a week. In 1947 he was offered a tryout with the Brooklyn dodgers. Before no African Americans had been allowed to participate in the minor or major leagues. After signing a contract, Jackie Robinson was sent to the minor leagues and there he played for one year with Montreal a team in the International League. Following a year in which he was the best hitter in the league he was brought up to the major leagues. During the first year 1947 he showed his greatness and was named the rookie of the year. Two years later he was the most valuable player in the national league and won the batting title with a .342 average. Despite the initial bigoted opposition by some baseball fans and players he performed with dignity courage and skill. Nevertheless he was an independent proud person. In the book Players of Cooperstown Mike Tully wrote he Robinson refused to be someone he was not, refused to conform to an image of a man who 'knew his place.' Because sports is such a high profile activity Jackie Robinson is credited with playing a significant role in breaking down the racial barriers in society. In his ten years in the major leagues he helped his team reach the world series six times. He was inducted into the Baseball hall of fame in 1962.

⁓ Chapter Review

Exercise 7   Writing Sentences with Correct Punctuation

Demonstrate your ability to use punctuation by writing sentences that contain these marks. Use the topics in parentheses.

Comma (travel)
1. To separate independent clauses in a compound sentence using a coordinating conjunction, FANBOYS (Use one: *for, and, nor, but, or, yet, so*) _____

   _____

2. For long introductory modifiers (Use one: *because, after, that, when, as, since, how, till, unless, before*, and others) _____

   _____

3. To separate words in a series _____

   _____

Semicolon (a family member)

4. To connect two related independent clauses without a coordinating conjunction _____

_____

Quotation Marks (Use this textbook as your source for quotations.)

5. To set off a quotation (words taken from the written work or the speech of others) _____

_____

Italics, shown by underlining (school)

6. To refer to a word or letter by its name _____

_____

7. For the title of a book _____

_____

Colon (a job)

8. To introduce a list _____

_____

Apostrophe (friendship)

9. To show a singular or plural possessive _____

_____

10. To write a contraction _____

_____

Hyphen (shopping)

11. To use in numbers _____

_____

12. To indicate two-word modifiers _____

_____

11

Spelling and Commonly Confused Words

 Spelling Tips

The following tips will help you become a better speller:

- **Do not omit letters.**

  Many errors occur because certain letters are omitted when the word is pronounced or spelled. Observe the omissions in the following words. Then concentrate on learning the correct spellings.

Incorrect	Correct	Incorrect	Correct
agravate	aggravate	ajourned	adjourned
aproved	approved	aquaintance	acquaintance
artic	arctic	comodity	commodity
efficent	efficient	envirnment	environment
familar	familiar	irigation	irrigation
libary	library	paralell	parallel
parlament	parliament	paticulaly	particularly
readly	readily	sophmore	sophomore
stricly	strictly	unconsious	unconscious

- **Do not add letters.**

Incorrect	Correct	Incorrect	Correct
athelete	athlete	comming	coming
drownded	drowned	folkes	folks
occassionally	occasionally	ommission	omission
pasttime	pastime	priviledge	privilege
similiar	similar	tradgedy	tragedy

178

- **Do not substitute incorrect letters for correct letters.**

Incorrect	Correct	Incorrect	Correct
benefi*s*ial	benefi*c*ial	bull*i*tins	bull*e*tins
*s*ensus	*c*ensus	d*i*scription	d*e*scription
d*e*sease	d*i*sease	dissen*t*ion	dissen*s*ion
it*i*ms	it*e*ms	offen*c*e	offen*s*e
peculi*e*r	peculi*a*r	re*s*itation	re*c*itation
scre*a*ch	scre*e*ch	substan*s*ial	substan*t*ial
surpri*z*e	surpri*s*e	techn*a*cal	techn*i*cal

- **Do not transpose letters.**

Incorrect	Correct	Incorrect	Correct
alu*nm*i	alu*mn*i	child*er*n	child*re*n
dup*il*cate	dup*li*cate	irrev*el*ant	irrev*le*ant
kind*el*	kind*le*	p*re*haps	p*er*haps
p*er*fer	p*re*fer	p*er*scription	p*re*scription
princip*el*s	princip*le*s	y*ei*ld	y*ie*ld

Note: Whenever you notice other words that fall into any one of these categories, add them to the list.

- **Apply the spelling rules for spelling *ei* and *ie* words correctly.**

Remember the poem?

> Use *i* before *e*
> Except after *c*
> Or when sounded as *a*
> As in *neighbor* and *weigh*.

i before e

achieve	belief	believe	brief
chief	field	grief	hygiene
niece	piece	pierce	relief
relieve	shield	siege	variety

Except after c

ceiling	conceit	conceive	deceit
deceive	perceive	receipt	receive

Exceptions: either, financier, height, leisure, neither, seize, species, weird.

*When sounded as **a***

deign	eight	feign	feint
freight	heinous	heir	neigh
neighbor	rein	reign	skein
sleigh	veil	vein	weigh

- **Apply the rules for dropping the final *e* or retaining the final *e* when a suffix is added.**

Words ending in a silent *e* usually drop the *e* before a suffix beginning with a vowel; for example, *accuse + -ing = accusing*. Some common suffixes beginning with a vowel are the following: *-able, -al, -age, -ary, -ation, -ence, -ing, -ion, -ous, -ure.*

admire + *-able* = admirable	arrive + *-al* = arrival
come + *-ing* = coming	explore + *-ation* = exploration
fame + *-ous* = famous	imagine + *-ary* = imaginary
locate + *-ion* = location	please + *-ure* = pleasure
plume + *-age* = plumage	precede + *-ence* = precedence

Exceptions: dye + -ing = dyeing (to distinguish it from *dying*), *acreage, mileage.*

Words ending in a silent *e* usually retain the *e* before a suffix beginning with a consonant; for example: *arrange + -ment = arrangement*. Some common suffixes beginning with a consonant are the following: *-craft, -ful, -less, -ly, -mate, -ment, -ness, -ty.*

entire + *-ty* = entirety	hate + *-ful* = hateful
hope + *-less* = hopeless	like + *-ness* = likeness
manage + *-ment* = management	safe + *-ly* = safely
stale + *-mate* = stalemate	state + *-craft* = statecraft

Exceptions: Some words taking the *-ful* or *-ly* suffixes drop the final *e*:

awe + *-ful* = awful	due + *-ly* = duly
true + *-ly* = truly	whole + *-ly* = wholly

Some words taking the suffix *-ment* drop the final *e*; for example:

acknowledgment	argument	judgment

Words ending in silent *e* after *c* or *g* retain the *e* when the suffix begins with the vowel *a* or *o*. The final *e* is retained to keep the *c* or *g* soft before the suffixes.

advantageous	courageous
noticeable	peaceable

- **Apply the rules for doubling a final consonant before a suffix beginning with a vowel.**

Words of one syllable

blot	blotted	brag	bragging	cut	cutting
drag	dragged	drop	dropped	get	getting
hop	hopper	hot	hottest	man	mannish
plan	planned	rob	robbed	run	running
sit	sitting	stop	stopped	swim	swimming

Words accented on the last syllable

acquit	acquitted	admit	admittance
allot	allotted	begin	beginning
commit	committee	concur	concurring
confer	conferring	defer	deferring
equip	equipped	occur	occurrence
omit	omitting	prefer	preferred
refer	referred	submit	submitted
transfer	transferred		

Words that are not accented on the last syllable or words that do not end in a single consonant preceded by a vowel do not double the final consonant (regardless of whether the suffix begins with a vowel).

⁓ Frequently Misspelled Words

absence	beginning	dependent	environment	government
across	belief	develop	especially	grammar
actually	benefit	development	etc.	grateful
all right	buried	difference	exaggerate	guarantee
a lot	business	disastrous	excellent	guard
among	certain	discipline	exercise	guidance
analyze	college	discussed	existence	height
appearance	coming	disease	experience	hoping
appreciate	committee	divide	explanation	humorous
argument	competition	dying	extremely	immediately
athlete	complete	eighth	familiar	independent
athletics	consider	eligible	February	intelligence
awkward	criticism	eliminate	finally	interest
becoming	definitely	embarrassed	foreign	interfere

involved	occasionally	prove	secretary	surprise
knowledge	opinion	psychology	senior	thoroughly
laboratory	opportunity	pursue	sense	though
leisure	parallel	receipt	separate	tragedy
length	particular	receive	severely	tried
library	persuade	recommend	shining	tries
likely	physically	reference	significant	truly
lying	planned	relieve	similar	unfortunately
marriage	pleasant	religious	sincerely	unnecessary
mathematics	possible	repetition	sophomore	until
meant	practical	rhythm	speech	unusual
medicine	preferred	ridiculous	straight	using
neither	prejudice	sacrifice	studying	usually
ninety	privilege	safety	succeed	Wednesday
ninth	probably	scene	success	writing
nuclear	professor	schedule	suggest	written

Exercise 1   Using Correct Spelling

Underline the misspelled words and write the correct spelling above the words. Double underline the words that are incorrectly spelled but would go unchallenged by your spell checker.

Professor Pufnagel was torturing his English students once again, and he relished his familar evil roll. "Today, class, we will write without the assistence of computers. In fact, never again will we use them in this class. They are a perscription for lazyness. And they make life to easy for alot of you."

The profesor lectured the students for an hour, stresing that when he was in school, there were no computers in his enviroment. He extoled the virtues of writting with little yellow pensils, fountain pens, and solid, dependible typewriters. He went on with his ranting, listing computer games, television sets, frozen foods, plastic wrap, asperin, and Velcro as similiar and familiar negative forces that had lead society to it's truely sorry state. "You are nothing but a pityful pack of party people, and you will recieve no sympathy from me," he sputtered. Grabbing a student's laptop computer, Pufnagel reared back and, like an athalete, hurled it against the wall. Soon, in the corner of the classroom lay a pile of high-tech junk, once fine shinning machines, now just garbage— smashed in a senseless, aweful war against technology.

The students starred in embarassed amazement at there professor, who was developing a nervous twitch. His mouth began twisting and contorting as his limbs jerked with the helter-skelter motion of a tangled marionette. He clutched desparately at his throat, and smoke began to poor out of his ears and neck. Unconsious, he crashed to the floor with a clatter.

One of the students, who had just taken a CPR class, rushed forward and attempted to revive the fallen educator. As the student pounded with a catchy rap rhythem on the chest of his stricken teacher, everyone herd a loud pop and sizzle.

It was a door in Pufnagel's chest, which had poped open to reveal the complex electrical control panel of a short-circuited cyborg!

Just than a security team in white jumpsuits from student goverment entered the class, carefully deposited Pufnagel on a wheelbarrow, and roled him out to the Faculty Service Center.

A few minutes later a Professor Ramirez arrived. "Ladys and gentlemen," she said, "its time to start your search engines. Your prevous professor's mainframe is down, but I'm his substitute and mine is fine, fine, fine, fine, fine, fine, fine, fine, fine, fine...."

∼ Confused Spelling / Confusing Words

The following are more words that are commonly misspelled or confused with one another. Some have similar sounds, some are often mispronounced, and some are only misunderstood.

a	An article adjective used before a word beginning with a consonant or a consonant sound, as in "I ate *a* donut."
an	An article adjective used before a word beginning with a vowel (*a, e, i, o, u*) or with a silent *h*, as in "I ate *an* artichoke."
and	A coordinating conjunction, as in "Sara *and* I like Johnny Cash."
accept	A verb meaning "to receive," as in "I *accept* your explanation."
except	A preposition meaning "to exclude," as in "I paid everyone *except* you."
advice	A noun meaning "guidance," as in "Thanks for the *advice*."
advise	A verb meaning "to give guidance," as in "Will you please *advise* me of my rights?"
all right	An adjective meaning "correct" or "acceptable," as in "It's *all right* to cry."
alright	Not used in formal writing.

all ready	An adjective that can be used interchangeably with *ready*, as in "I am *all ready* to go to town."
already	An adverb meaning "before," which cannot be used in place of *ready*, as in "I have *already* finished."
a lot	An adverb meaning "much," as in "She liked him *a lot*," or a noun meaning "several," as in "I had *a lot* of suggestions."
alot	Misspelling.
altogether	An adverb meaning "completely," as in "He is *altogether* happy."
all together	An adverb meaning "as one," which can be used interchangeably with *together*, as in "The group left *all together*."
could of	Misspelling.
could have	A verb phrase, as in "I *could have* used some kindness."
choose	A present-tense verb meaning "to select," as in "Do whatever you *choose*."
chose	The past-tense form of the verb *choose*, as in "They *chose* to take action yesterday."
effect	Usually a noun meaning "result," as in "That *effect* was unexpected."
affect	Usually a verb meaning "change," as in "Ideas *affect* me."
hear	A verb indicating the receiving of sound, as in "I *hear* thunder."
here	An adverb meaning "present location," as in "I live *here*."
it's	A contraction of *it is*, as in "*It's* time to dance."
its	Possessive pronoun, as in "Each dog has *its* day."
know	A verb usually meaning "to comprehend" or "to recognize," as in "I *know* the answer."
no	An adjective meaning "negative," as in "I have *no* potatoes."
led	The past-tense form of the verb *lead*, as in "I *led* a wild life in my youth."

lead	A present-tense verb, as in "I *lead* a stable life now" or a noun referring to a substance, such as "I sharpened the *lead* in my pencil."
loose	An adjective meaning "without restraint," as in "He is a *loose* cannon."
lose	A present-tense verb from the pattern *lose, lost, lost,* as in "I thought I would *lose* my senses."
paid	The past tense form of *pay,* as in "He *paid* his dues."
payed	Misspelling.
passed	The past-tense form of the verb *pass,* meaning "went by," as in "He *passed* me on the curve."
past	An adjective meaning "former," as in "That's *past* history"; or a noun, as in "the *past.*"
patience	A noun meaning "willingness to wait," as in "Job was a man of much *patience.*"
patients	A noun meaning "people under care," as in "The doctor had fifty *patients.*"
peace	A noun meaning "a quality of calmness" or "absence of strife," as in "The guru was at *peace* with the world."
piece	A noun meaning "part," as in "I gave him a *piece* of my mind."
quiet	An adjective meaning "silent," as in "She was a *quiet* child."
quit	A verb meaning "to cease" or "to withdraw," as in "I *quit* my job."
quite	An adverb meaning "very," as in "The clam is *quite* happy."
receive	A verb meaning "to accept," as in "I will *receive* visitors now."
recieve	Misspelling.
stationary	An adjective meaning "not moving," as in "Try to avoid running into *stationary* objects."
stationery	A noun meaning "paper material to write on," as in "I bought a box of *stationery* for Sue's birthday present."
than	A conjunction, as in "He is taller *than* I am."
then	An adverb, as in "She *then* left town."
their	An adjective, as in "They read *their* books."

there	An adverb, as in "He left it *there*," or a filler word as in "*There* is no time left."
they're	A contraction of *they are*, as in "*They're* happy."
to	A preposition, as in "I went *to* town."
too	An adverb meaning "having exceeded or gone beyond what is acceptable," as in "You are *too* late to qualify for the discount," or "also," as in "I have feelings, *too*."
two	An adjective of number, as in "I have *two* jobs."
thorough	An adjective, as in "He did a *thorough* job."
through	A preposition, as in "She went *through* the yard."
truly	An adverb meaning "sincerely" or "completely," as in "He was *truly* happy."
truely	Misspelling.
weather	A noun meaning "condition of the atmosphere," as in "The *weather* is pleasant today."
whether	A conjunction, as in "*Whether* he would go was of no consequence."
write	A present-tense verb, as in "Watch me as I *write* this letter."
writen	Misspelling.
written	A past-participle verb, as in "I have *written* the letter."
you're	A contraction of *you are*, as in "*You're* my friend."
your	A possessive pronoun, as in "I like *your* looks."

Exercise 2   Spelling Confusing Words

Underline the correct word or words.

1. I cannot (hear, here) the answers.

2. Isabella is taller (then, than) I.

3. They left town to find (their, they're, there) roots.

4. Sam went (through, thorough) the initiation.

5. I am only asking for a little (peace, piece) of the action.

6. Whatever you say is (alright, all right) with me.

7. I (passed, past) the test, and now I'm ready for action.

8. That smash was (to, too, two) hot to handle.

9. I did not ask for her (advise, advice).

10. I found (a lot, alot) of new ideas in that book.

11. Marilyn has (all ready, already) left.

12. I (chose, choose) my answer and hoped for the best.

13. I knew that I would (recieve, receive) fair treatment.

14. Juan was (quit, quite, quiet) happy with my decision.

15. Maria (could of, could have) completed the assignment.

16. Marlin knew they would (lose, loose) the game.

17. I've heard that (it's, its) a good movie.

18. June would not (accept, except) my answer.

19. I did not (know, no) what to do.

20. Sean (paid, payed) his bill and left town.

Exercise 3   Spelling Confusing Words

Underline the correct word or words.

1. Erin said that my application was (alright, all right).

2. Sheriff Andy Griffith worked hard for (peace, piece) in Mayberry.

3. Lauren was the first woman to (recieve, receive) a medal.

4. Shane spoke his mind; (then, than) he left.

5. The cleaners did a (through, thorough) job.

6. After the loud explosion, there was (quit, quiet, quite).

7. The nurse worked diligently with his (patience, patients).

8. They were not (altogether, all together) happy, but they (could of, could have) been.

9. The cowboys (led, lead) the cows to water.

10. For my hobby, I study (grammar, grammer).

11. Elvis (truly, truely) respected his mother.

12. Jarrett asked for the (whether, weather) report.

13. I never (advise, advice) my friends about gambling.

14. You should (accept, except) responsibility for your actions.

15. Matthew inherited (alot, a lot) of money.

16. We waited for the gorilla to (chose, choose) a mate.

17. Virginia thinks (its, it's) a good day for a party.

18. It was a tale of (to, too, two) cities.

19. I went (they're, their, there) to my childhood home.

20. It was the best letter Kevin had ever (writen, written, wrote).

∾ Wordy Phrases

Certain phrases clutter sentences, consuming our time in writing and our readers' time in reading. Watch for wordy phrases as you revise and edit your composition.

WORDY *Due to the fact* that he was unemployed, he had to use public transportation.

CONCISE *Because* he was unemployed, he had to use public transportation.

WORDY *Deep down inside* he believed that the Red Sox would win.

CONCISE He believed that the Red Sox would win.

Wordy	Concise
at the present time	now
basic essentials	essentials
blend together	blend
it is clear that	(delete)
due to the fact that	because
for the reason that	because
I felt inside	I felt
in most cases	usually
as a matter of fact	in fact
in the event that	if
until such time as	until
I personally feel	I feel
in this modern world	today
in order to	to
most of the people	most people
along the lines of	like
past experience	experience
at that point in time	then
in the final analysis	finally
in the near future	soon
have a need for	need
in this day and age	now

Exercise 4 Avoiding Wordy Phrasing

Circle the wordy phrases and write in concise phrases.

1. I tried to recall that moment, but my memories seemed to

   blend together.

2. I expect to get out of this bed and go to work in the near future.

3. As a matter of fact, when I was a child, I had an imaginary playmate.

4. I feel in my heart that bees work too hard.

5. I am not surprised by his conviction due to the fact that as a child he used to torment vegetables.

6. In this modern world most of the people do not use enough shoe polish.

7. I was crowned Mr. Clean for the reason that I always wash my hands before I wash my hands.

8. At the present time I am concentrating on not thinking about warthogs.

9. Procrastination is an idea I will consider in the near future.

10. I personally feel that Cupid just shot me with a poisoned arrow.

12

The Writing Process: Paragraphs and Essays

～ The Paragraph and Essay Defined

A typical **paragraph** is a group of sentences that relate to a single idea. That idea, called the **controlling idea**, is often stated in one sentence, which is known as the **topic sentence**. All the other sentences in the paragraph explain or support the topic sentence.

An **essay** contains multiple paragraphs. It begins with an **introductory paragraph** that usually presents the main idea (or **thesis**). The main idea is then developed in several paragraphs that make up the **body of the essay**, and those parts are often linked with transitional words and may be joined with transitional paragraphs. An essay usually ends with a concluding paragraph that gives an impression of finality, or closure. The **concluding paragraph** sometimes summarizes the main idea that was developed throughout the essay; it may answer a question that was posed at the beginning of the essay; and usually does reflect back on the thesis of the essay.

Considered structurally, the paragraph is often an essay in miniature. That does not mean that all paragraphs can grow up to be essays or that all essays can shrink to become paragraphs. For college writing, however, a good understanding of the parallel between well-organized paragraphs and well-organized essays is useful. As you learn the properties of effective paragraphs—those with a strong topic sentence and strong support—you also learn how to organize an essay, if you just magnify the procedure.

Thus, paragraphs can come in different shapes and sizes. The length of a paragraph varies. It can be as short as part of a word (in a paragraph of dialogue). Or it can be pages long. It should be long enough to develop the controlling idea of the writer. If it is the answer to a "short essay" part of a test, it may be called a **stand-alone paragraph**; therefore, it is sometimes treated or regarded as a short essay, though it is

192

indented only once. Some featured paragraphs in this book and those in the other books in the *At a Glance* series are ordinary paragraphs for longer works, and some are stand-alone paragraphs. As you look at them without a context, it may be difficult to determine the kind, but each kind is developed with the same principle: "State your idea and support it." A paragraph of development in an essay should extend in proportion to the whole essay, depending on its purpose and audience. A stand-alone paragraph should be as long as needed to convey all the necessary information, which will depend on the situation and, specifically, the assignment. It is not unusual for instructors to prescribe the length or range of paragraph assignments.

The following diagram illustrates the parallel parts of many outlines, paragraphs, and essays:

PARAGRAPH	OUTLINE	ESSAY
Topic Sentence	Topic Sentence or Thesis	Introduction, with Thesis or Purpose
Support Sentence 1	I. Support 1	
Support Sentence 2	II. Support 2	Support Paragraph 1
Support Sentence 3	III. Support 3	Support Paragraph 2
Concluding Sentence	Conclusion	Support Paragraph 3
		Conclusion

⌒ The Writing Process

Effective and easily followed steps exist for writing a paragraph and even an essay. Writing does not mean merely putting words on a piece of paper. It is a process that often involves several stages: using prewriting techniques to explore a topic; limiting and then developing the topic, usually with an outline; writing a first draft; revising the draft as often as necessary; and editing the material. At times, writers discover that their topic sentence or their outline does not work, and they go back and alter their original concept or design.

Here is how one student, Vera Harris, moved from an idea to a topic sentence to an outline to a paragraph. Vera Harris returned to college while she still had a full-time job as a hairdresser. When her instructor asked her to write a paragraph about types of people she had encountered, she naturally considered her customers for the subject of her paragraph—what she would write about. But she also had a special interest in dogs, and she hoped she would be able, somehow, to include that interest. Although she knew her topic rather well, she worked with some prewriting techniques that allowed her to get her ideas flowing onto paper.

Prewriting

Freewriting

Vera wrote about a page without stopping, just letting her ideas tumble forward without concern for correctness. This enabled her to get her project under way and to deal immediately with the common problem of writer's block. She knew that most of the material would be unusable, but she also knew that she would probably hit on some good ideas that would give her a sense of direction and new insights. These good ideas she would circle and perhaps even make notes about in the margins of her paper. Here is Vera's freewriting:

> I have worked in beauty shops for a long time and I've naturally made a lot of observations about my customers. I could write about what they look like and how they behave and how they tip and lots of things. When I first started to work I guess at first I thought of them as pretty much the same but then I started to see them as types mainly as to how they acted and I remember way back then I sometimes thought of how they reminded me of dogs. I don't mean that in any bad way but just that human beings have their personalities and their appearances and all and so do dogs.

Brainstorming

Vera then sharpened her focus by listing some words and phrases, mainly in response to the questions *Who? What? Where? When? Why?* and *How?* One (*How?*) became a list.

> *Who?* my customers
> *What?* the way they act
> *Where?* in the beauty salon
> *When?* for the years I have worked
> *Why?* their basic nature
> *How?* behavior sometimes like dogs—hounds, Dobermans, terriers, bulldogs, cockers, poodles, mixed, retrievers, boxers

Clustering

After indicating her main subject inside a double bubble, Vera jotted down ideas inside single bubbles radiating out from the topic hub, as shown in the following cluster. With this arrangement, she could begin to see connections.

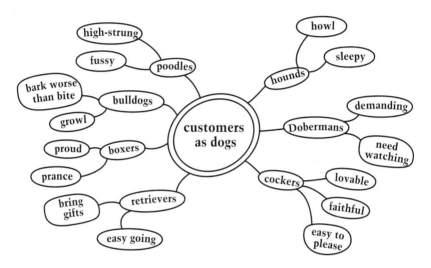

Topic Sentence

At that point, knowing her subject material and the assignment very well, Vera wrote a topic sentence. A **topic sentence** controls the paragraph by indicating the subject (what the writer is writing about) and the focus (what the writer is doing with the subject) of the subject.

The customers in the beauty shop where I work
subject

remind me of types of dogs (of which I am fond).
focus

Outline

Then Vera made a basic outline. An **outline** is a pattern for showing the relationship of ideas. Vera supported her topic sentence by listing the types of dogs her customers reminded her of. Under each type, she described the characteristics typical of both the dogs and the people. The major-support and minor-support labels show you how she organized her material in correct outline form.

TOPIC SENTENCE   The customers in the beauty shop where I work remind me of types of dogs (of which I am fond).

I. Poodles (major support)
   A. High-strung (minor support)
   B. Need attention (minor support)
II. Doberman pinschers (major support)
   A. Demanding (minor support)
   B. Need watching (minor support)
III. Bulldogs (major support)
   A. Act mean (minor support)
   B. Will back down (minor support)
IV. Cocker spaniels (major support)
   A. Lovable (minor support)
   B. Faithful (minor support)
   C. Easy to please (minor support)

If Vera had experienced problems, she would have gone back to her topic sentence or even to her prewriting to make adjustments.

Writing a First Draft

Following her outline for her main and supporting points, Vera wrote her first draft. (With more development, this writing could have been a six-paragraph essay instead of a long paragraph. See the diagram on page 193.) In a first draft, writers do not try to "get everything right." They try to discuss the topic as fully as possible. Here is Vera's first draft:

```
               Customers Are Like Canines

        I have worked in a beauty salon for a long time.
   There, I have come across almost every kind of salon
   customer, each with her own unique looks and personality.
   I am also a dog lover and I have observed numerous
   dogs with care it is easier to classify these people
   if I compare them with canine types—but in a playful
   rather than a mean way. The first group is made up of
   poodles. Poodles are very prissy, with a constant need
   for attention. Their hair is usually over-styled. They
   think puffballs in soft colors look great. The next
   group and largest group is made up of cocker spanieals.
```

> The Cockers are very lovable the most faithful. They
> like being pampered. Cockers like to see me every week
> and visit with others. Sometimes I can almost see their
> tails wagging. Then come the Doberman pinchers, this type
> scares me the most. Dobies are hard to please. If one
> hair goes the wrong way. I will see their upper lip rise
> up to show eyeteeth, as if they are snarling. I rarely
> turn my back while working on this type—a Dobie might
> bite. The last group the bulldogs, are not as mean as
> Dobies Bulldogs act mean and tough, but if you don't show
> fear when they get bossy they will back down. This type
> needs to feel in charge, even if it's me leading them
> around on a leash.

Revising and Editing with the Brandon Guide

After writing her first draft, Vera began revising her paragraph. To revise is to rearrange and polish the writing, putting the sentences in the best possible order and coming up with the best possible words. Vera used the acronym CLUESS to remember her revision checklist:

> Coherence: Does the material flow smoothly from each idea, leading logically and evenly to the next?
>
> Language: Are the words appropriate for the message, occasion, and audience (avoiding slang, clichés, and worn-out expressions)?
>
> Unity: Are all the ideas related and subordinate to the topic sentence?
>
> Emphasis: Are techniques such as repetition and careful placement of words and ideas used to emphasize the main points?
>
> Support: Do details, examples, and similar material back up, justify, or prove the topic sentence?
>
> Sentences: Is there some variety in sentence structure?

Finally, Vera edited her paper. To edit is to correct the basic writing errors that have been overlooked. Vera used the acronym CGPS to remember the one question that would cover her concerns: Are there problems with capitalization, grammar, punctuation, and spelling?

The properties of these two acronyms—CLUESS and CGPS—create a system of writing called the Brandon Guide to Revising and Editing.

Here is Vera's first draft, revised and edited:

```
          Customers Are Like Canines
```

language punctuation	*Over the years while working* ~~I have worked~~ in a beauty salon ∧ ~~for a~~
	~~long time. There,~~ I have come across almost
	every kind of salon customer, each with her
sentences	own unique looks and personality. ∧*Because* I am also a
	dog lover and ~~I~~ have observed numerous dogs
punctuation	with care ∧ it is easier to classify these
language	people if I ∧*relate them to* ~~compare them with~~ canine types—
logic	but in a playful rather than a mean way. The
	first group is made up of poodles. Poodles
language	are very prissy ∧*and high-strung*, with a constant need for
	attention. Their hair is usually over⌒styled.
	They think puffballs in soft colors look
emphasis spelling omission	great. The *last* ~~next group~~ and largest group, is
	made up of cocker spani*e*ls. The ¢ockers are
language	very lovable ∧*and* the most faithful. They ~~like~~*enjoy*
	being ~~pampered.~~*groomed and stroked, but they are easy to please.* Cockers like to see me every
	week and ∧*to* visit with others. Sometimes I can
	almost see their tails wagging. Then come the
sentences	Doberman pincher*s*s∘∧ ᵀ*T*his type scares me the
```
```

most. Dobies are hard to please. If one hair

sentences   goes the wrong way͵ I will see their upper lip

language   rise up to ~~show~~ ᴀexpose eyeteeth⸰ ~~as if they are~~

~~snarling,~~ I rarely turn my back while working

punctuation   on this type⸍a Dobie might bite. The ~~last~~ ᴀthird–

members,
group ᴀthe bulldogs, are not as mean as Dobies⸰

language   Bulldogs act mean and tough, but if ~~you don't~~ ᴀone doesn't

punctuation   show fear when they get bossyᴀ they will back

down. This type needs to feel in charge, even

language   if ~~it's me~~ ᴀI'm leading them around on a leash.͵
No matter what, canines and customers are my best friends.

Here is Vera's final draft:

Customers Are Like Canines

topic sentence   Over the years while working in a beauty
salon, I have come across almost every kind
of salon customer, each with her own unique
looks and personality. Because I am also a
dog lover and have observed numerous dogs
with care, it is easier to classify these
support   people if I relate them to canine types—but
in a playful rather than a mean way. The
first group is made up of poodles. Poodles
are very prissy and high-strung, with a
constant need for attention. Their hair is
usually overstyled. They think puffballs
support   in soft colors look great. Then come the

Doberman pinschers. This type scares me the most. Dobies are hard to please. If one hair goes the wrong way, I will see their upper lip rise up to expose eyeteeth. I rarely turn **support** my back while working on this type—a Dobie might bite. The third-group members, the bulldogs, are not as mean as Dobies. Bulldogs act mean and tough, but if one doesn't show fear when they get bossy, they will back down. This type needs to feel in charge, even **support** if I'm leading them around on a leash. The last—and largest—group is made up of cocker spaniels. The cockers are very lovable and the most faithful. They enjoy being groomed and stroked, but they are easy to please. Cockers like to see me every week and to visit with others. Sometimes I can almost see their tails wagging. No matter what, canines and customers are my best friends.

The Brandon Writing Process Worksheet

The Brandon Writing Process Worksheet on page A-2 (and also in an enlarged form on your Student Companion Site online at www.cengagebrain.com) can help you move smoothly from assignment to the final paragraph or essay. Your instructor may ask you to complete the worksheet and submit it for topic approval during prewriting or with your final paper to document how you proceeded.

Using the check boxes on the worksheet will help you write step by step, going back and forth when you need to do so, and not overlooking key parts of the writing process.

13

Writing a Summary

A summary is a rewritten, shortened version of a piece of writing in which you use mostly your words to express the main ideas presented in the original piece. Learning to summarize effectively will help you in many ways. Summary writing reinforces comprehension skills in reading. It requires you to discriminate among the ideas in the target reading passage. A summary can be written in the form of a well-designed paragraph. Frequently, summaries are used in collecting material for research papers and in writing conclusions to essays.

The following rules will guide you in writing effective summaries.

1. Cite both the author and the title of the text.
2. Reduce the length of the original by about two-thirds, although the exact reduction will vary depending on the content of the original.
3. Concentrate on the main ideas and include details only infrequently.
4. Change the original wording without changing the idea.
5. Do not evaluate the content or give an opinion in any way (even if you see an error in logic or fact).
6. Do not add ideas (even if you have an abundance of related information).
7. Do not include any personal comments (that is, do not use *I*, referring to self).
8. Use quotations only infrequently. (If you do use quotations, enclose them in quotation marks.)
9. Use author tags ("says York," "according to York," or "the author explains") to remind the reader that you are summarizing the material of another writer.
10. Begin with the main idea (as you usually do in middle paragraphs) and cover the main points in an organized fashion while using complete sentences.

Now look at "The Roman Toga," a short passage from a history textbook. A student, Leon Batista, underlined (drawing lines under selective parts) and annotated it (writing interpretive phrases in margins) to indicate important ideas and then summarized the passage.

The Roman Toga

toga, mostly impractical

1   Practicality has never been a requirement of fashion. The Roman toga was an uncomfortable garment. It was hot in summer, cold in winter, and clumsy for just about any activity but standing still. The toga was,

practical, "easy to make"

however, practical in one way: It was easy to make, since it involved no sewing. Not even a buttonhole was needed. An adult's toga

"wool blanket"

was basically a large wool blanket measuring about 18 by 7 feet. It was draped around the body in a variety of ways without the use of buttons or pins.

fashions changed for woman, not much for men

2   In the early days of the Roman republic, both women and men wore togas. Women eventually wore more dresslike garments, called *stolas*, with separate shawls. For men, however, the toga remained in fashion with very little change.

togas symbol of Roman citizenship for males

3   Soon after the republic was formed, the toga became a symbol of Roman citizenship. Different styles of togas indicated a male citizen's place in society. For example, a young boy would wear a white toga with a narrow purple band along the border. When

"place in society" toga white with purple band

his family decided he was ready for adult responsibilities, he would don a pure white toga. On that day, usually when he was

in youth
white as adult

about 16, his family would take him to the Forum, where he would register as a full citizen. For the rest of his life, he would wear a toga at the theater, in court, for

wore to
theater, court,
religious
ceremony,
own funeral

religious ceremonies, and on any formal occasion. At his funeral his body would be wrapped in a toga to mark him, even in death, as a Roman citizen.

(Source: Adapted from Steven L. Jantzen, *World History: Perspectives on the Past*, pp. 79-80)

Summary of "The Roman Toga"
Leon Batista

According to Steven Jantzen in *World History: Perspectives on the Past*, the toga was the main form of dress for citizens of the Roman republic, despite its being "hot in summer, cold in winter, and clumsy" to wear. Perhaps the Romans appreciated the simplicity of wearing a piece of woolen cloth about eighteen by seven feet "without the use of buttons or pins." Jantzen explains that the women also wore another garment similar to a dress called the *stola*, but Roman male citizens were likely to wear only the toga—white with a purple edge for the young and solid white for the adult. This apparel was worn from childhood to death.

Exercise 1 Evaluating a Summary

Compare the following summary with the original passage and with the student summary you just read. Then mark the instances of poor summary writing by underlining and by using rule numbers from the list on page 201.

Summary About One of My Favorite Garments

For citizens of the Roman republic, the toga was the main form of dress, despite its being hot in summer, cold in winter, and clumsy to wear. Frankly, I don't see why a bright bunch of people like the Romans couldn't have come up with a better design. Perhaps the Romans appreciated the simplicity of wearing a piece of woolen cloth about eighteen by seven feet without buttons or pins, but I've read elsewhere that the togas were sometimes stolen at the public baths. The women also wore another garment similar to a dress called the *stola,* but the Roman male citizen was likely to wear only the toga—white with a purple edge for the young and solid white for the adult. For the rest of his life, he would wear a toga at the theater, in court, for religious ceremonies, and on any formal occasion. At his funeral, his body would be wrapped in a toga to mark him, even in death, as a Roman citizen.

14

Combined and Specific Patterns of Writing and Writing Topics

〜 Combined Patterns of Writing

Organization in a sound paragraph or essay reflects the intention of the author in fulfilling the needs of a writing task. As that writer, you begin by asking yourself what you are trying to say and who your audience is. If you are attempting to compare and contrast subject material, such as generations or leaders, then a comparative pattern of writing will prevail, providing a framework for your thoughts. If your objective is to show the causes of something, perhaps a trend or an event, then a discernible pattern of causes is likely to emerge in your writing.

Patterns can help you organize your thoughts so that your audience can easily understand your message. Each pattern is a collection of strategies for achieving certain purposes. Patterns are especially useful at the workplace when you need to respond succinctly according to a company-honored format or in a college essay test when your work must be done with an oppressive clock ticking and then evaluated by instructors overloaded with bluebooks.

Two cautionary points are worth considering:

- If the strategies are used in a strictly formulaic manner, the result may be mechanical and uninteresting. Fleshing out your ideas with explanation will usually submerge patterns of writing.
- It is uncommon for a single pattern to be used alone, and you would seldom attempt to do so. You cannot write a comparison-and-contrast essay without analyzing your content through division, and you might very well use definitions and examples.

Therefore, a well-written essay is usually a combination of different patterns from the ten or so available to you.

205

Point of view indicates how the author relates to the content. It will be either **first person** (from the *I, me, our,* or *we* perspective), **second person** (from the *you* perspective) or **third person** (from the *he, she, it,* or *they* perspective). Viewpoints are seldom mixed, and most academic writing is third person.

∿ Specific Patterns of Writing

Descriptive Narration

1. Include these points so that you will be sure you have a complete narrative:

   - situation (what's going on)
   - conflict (problem to be dealt with)
   - struggle (dealing with problem)
   - outcome (result of dealing with problem)
   - meaning (significance or point)

2. Use description to enhance and support your narration. A good descriptive writer presents material so that the perceptive reader can read and reexperience the writer's ideas. One device important to that writer is imagery. Images can be perceived through the senses (sight, sound, taste, smell, and touch). A good descriptive writer also gives specific details and presents concrete particulars (actual things) in a convincing way. We read, we visualize, we identify, and—*zap!*—we connect with a narrative account.

3. Use dialogue as appropriate.

4. Consider using the following transitional words to improve coherence by connecting ideas with ideas, sentences with sentences, and paragraphs with paragraphs:

   - **For description—Place:** *above, over, under, below, nearby, near, across, beyond, among, to the right, to the left, in the background, in the foreground, further, beside, opposite, within sight, out of sight*
   - **For narration—Time:** *after, before, later, earlier, initially, soon, recently, next, today, tomorrow, yesterday, now, then, until, currently, when, finally, not long after, immediately, (at) first, (at) last, third, previously, in the meantime, meanwhile*

5. Give details concerning action.

6. Be consistent with point of view (use *I* for first person or *he, she,* or *it* for third person) and verb tense (use *is* for present and *was* for past).
7. Keep in mind that most narratives written as college assignments will have an expository purpose; that is, they explain a specific idea.
8. Consider working with a limited time frame for short writing assignments; that is, the scope would usually be no more than one incident of brief duration for one paragraph. For example, writing about an entire graduation ceremony might be too complicated, but concentrating on the moment when you walked forward to receive the diploma or the moment when the relatives and friends come down on the field could work very well in a single paragraph.

General Topics

Each of the following topics concerns the writing of a descriptive narrative with meaning beyond the story itself. The narrative will be used to inform or to persuade in relation to a clearly stated idea.

1. Write a narrative based on a topic sentence such as this: "One experience showed me what _____ [pain, fear, anger, love, sacrifice, dedication, joy, sorrow, shame, pride] was really like."
2. Write a simple narrative about a fire, a riot, an automobile accident, a rescue, shoplifting, or some other unusual happening you witnessed.

Exemplification

1. Use examples to explain, convince, or amuse.
2. Use examples that are vivid, specific, and representative.

   - Vivid examples (the most colorful or memorable from your list of possible examples) attract attention.
   - Specific examples (such as names of places, things, and people) are identifiable.
   - Representative examples (those that are recognizable to readers) are typical and therefore the basis for generalization.

3. Tie your examples clearly to your thesis and your main points.
4. Draw your examples from what you have read, heard, and experienced.
5. Brainstorm a list or cluster of possible examples before you write.

6. Choose the order (time, place, or emphasis) and number of your examples according to the purpose stated in your topic sentence or thesis.
7. Consider using the following transitional words to improve coherence by connecting ideas with ideas, sentences with sentences, and paragraphs with paragraphs.

- *for example, as an example, another example, for instance, such as, including, specifically, especially, in particular, to illustrate, as an illustration, that is, i.e.* (meaning *that is*), *e.g.* (meaning *for example*)

General Topics

Make a judgmental statement about an issue you believe in strongly and then use one or more examples to illustrate your point. These are some possible topics:

1. high price of groceries
2. practical car(s) for family
3. property owners with(out) pride
4. violent computer games
5. good (or bad) role model(s)
6. pet peeve: drivers who break laws
7. bad job(s)
8. true friend(s)

Analysis by Division

Almost anything can be analyzed by division—for example, how the parts of the ear work in hearing, how the parts of the eye work in seeing, or how the parts of the heart work in pumping blood throughout the body. Subjects such as these are all approached with the same systematic procedure.

1. This is the procedure.

   - Step 1: Begin with something that is a unit.
   - Step 2: State the principle by which the unit can function.
   - Step 3: Divide the unit into parts according to that principle.
   - Step 4: Discuss each of the parts in relation to the unit.

2. This is the way you might apply that procedure to a good boss.

   - Unit: Manager
   - Principle of function: Effective as a leader
   - Parts based on the principle: Fair, intelligent, stable, competent in field
   - Discussion: Consider each part in relation to the person's effectiveness as a manager.

3. This is how a basic outline of analysis by division might look.

   Thesis: To be effective as a leader, a manager needs specific qualities.

      I. Fairness
     II. Intelligence
    III. Stability
    IV. Competence in the field

4. Consider using the following transitional words to improve coherence by connecting ideas with ideas, sentences with sentences, and paragraphs with paragraphs.

   - **Time or Numbering:** *first, second ,third, another, last, finally, soon, later, currently, before, along with, another part (section, component)*
   - **Space:** *above, below, to the left, to the right, near, beyond, under, next to, in the background, split, divide*
   - **Emphasis:** *most important(ly), equally important, central to the, to this end, as a result, taken collectively, with this purpose in mind, working with the, in fact, of course, above all, most of all, especially, primarily, without question*

General Topics

Some of the following topics are too broad for a short writing assignment and should be narrowed. For example, the general "a wedding ceremony" could be narrowed to the particular: "José and Maria's wedding ceremony." Divide your focused topic into parts and analyze it.

1. a wedding, a graduation, a religious ceremony, a holiday, a religious revival
2. a family, a relationship, a gang, a club, a sorority, or a fraternity
3. an album, a performance, a song, a singer, an actor, a musical group
4. a movie, a television program, a video game

Process Analysis

1. Decide whether your process analysis is mainly **directive** (how to do something) or **informative** (how you did something or how something occurred). Be consistent in using pronouns and other designations.

- For the directive process analysis, use the second person, addressing the reader as *you*. The *you* may be understood, in the case where it is not written.
- For the informative process analysis, use the first person, speaking as *I* or *we*, or the third person, speaking about the subject as *he, she, it,* or *they,* or by name.

2. Consider using these basic forms: directive process analysis or informative process analysis.

Directive Process Analysis

I. Preparation

   A.

   B.

II. Steps

   A.

   B.

   C.

How to Prepare Spring Rolls

  I. Preparation

    A. Suitable cooking area

    B. Utensils, equipment

    C. Spring-roll wrappers

    D. Vegetables, sauce

  II. Steps

    A. Season vegetables

    B. Wrap vegetables

    C. Fold wrappers

    D. Deep fry rolls

    E. Serve rolls with sauce

Informative Process Analysis

I. Background

   A.

   B.

II. Sequence

   A.

   B.

   C.

How Coal Is Formed

  I. Background or context

    A. Accumulation of land

    B. Plants

    C. Bacterial action

    D. Muck formation

  II. Sequence

    A. Lignite from pressure

    B. Bituminous from deep burial and heat

    C. Anthracite from metamorphic conditions

3. Create a list, beginning with the Roman-numeral headings indicated in item 2.
4. Determine the order of process analysis. It will usually be chronological (based on time).
5. Consider using the following transitional words to improve coherence by connecting ideas with ideas, sentences with sentences, and paragraphs with paragraphs.

- **Preparation and Background:** *at the outset, before stages develop, before steps occur, before work begins, as preparation for, in anticipation of, in laying the groundwork*
- **Steps and Stages:** *first, second, third, another step, next, now, then, at this point, at this stage, at this step, after, at last, finally, subsequently, to begin with, initially, after that, afterward, at the same time, concurrently, meanwhile, soon, during the process, during …, in order to, for a minute, for a …*

General Topics

Most of the following topics are directive as they are phrased. However, each can be transformed into a how-it-was-done informative topic by personalizing it and explaining stage by stage how you, someone else, or a group did something. For example, you could write either a directive process analysis about how to deal with an obnoxious person or an informative process analysis about how you or someone else dealt with an obnoxious person. Keep in mind that the two types of process analysis are often blended, especially in the personal approach. Many of the following topics will be more interesting to you and your readers if they are personalized.

Select one of the following topics and write a process-analysis paragraph or essay about it. Most of the topics require some narrowing to be treated in a paragraph. For example, writing about playing baseball is too broad; writing about how to throw a curve ball may be manageable.

- How to pass a test for a driver's license, get a job at a specific place, cook a food, eat a food, fix an appliance, fix a sprinkler, change a tire on a car, assemble an item, wrap a package, repair clothing, perform a task at work, perform a task at home, paint a house, or change a diaper

Cause and Effect

1. Determine whether your topic should mainly inform or mainly persuade, and use the right tone for your purpose and audience.

2. Use listing to brainstorm cause-and-effect ideas. This is an effective form of prewriting.

Causes	Event, Situation, or Trend	Effects
Low self-esteem	*Joining a gang*	Life of crime
Drugs		Drug addiction
Tradition		Surrogate family
Fear		relationship
Needs surrogate family		Protection
Wants protection		Ostracism
Neighborhood status		Restricted vocational opportunities

3. Decide whether to concentrate on causes, effects, or a combination of causes and effects. Most paragraphs will focus only on causes or only on effects. Many short essays will discuss causes and effects but will use one as the framework for the piece. A typical basic outline might look like this:

Topic sentence of paragraph or thesis of essay
  I. Cause (or Effect) 1
  II. Cause (or Effect) 2
  III. Cause (or Effect) 3

4. Do not conclude that something is an effect merely because it follows something else in time. For example, a recession after the election of a new leader may or may not be an effect of the election.
5. Lend emphasis to your main concern(s)—causes, effects, or a combination—by repeating key words such as *cause, reason, effect, result, consequence,* and *outcome.*
6. Keep in mind that causes and effects can be primary (main) or secondary (contributing), immediate or remote.
7. Base the order of causes and effects in your paper on time, space, emphasis, or a combination.
8. Consider using the following transitional words to improve coherence by connecting ideas with ideas, sentences with sentences, and paragraphs with paragraphs.

   ■ **Cause:** *as, because, because of, due to, for, for the reason that, since, bring about, another cause, for this reason, one cause, a second cause, another cause, a final cause*

- **Effect:** *accordingly, finally, consequently, hence, so, therefore, thus, as a consequence, as a result, resulting*

General Topics

Select one of the topics in the following list as a subject (situation, circumstance, or trend) for your paragraph or essay and then determine whether you will concentrate on causes, effects, or a combination. You can probably write a more interesting, well-developed, and therefore successful paragraph or essay on a topic you can personalize. If you do not personalize the topic, you will probably have to do some basic research to supply details for development.

1. attending or completing college
2. change in policy at work or school
3. alcoholism, any addiction
4. moving to another country, state, or home
5. passing or failing a test or course
6. having or getting a job
7. change in coaches, teachers
8. gambling
9. exercising, dieting
10. teenage marriage or parenthood

Classification

1. Follow this procedure for writing paragraphs and essays of classification:

   - Select a plural subject.

     Bosses

   - Decide on a principle for grouping the units of the subject.

     Their management style (the way they treat employees)

   - Establish the classes (groups)
   - Dictator, Cunning Manipulator, Buddy, Democratic Director
   - For subclasses, clearly indicate the different levels or characteristics. An outline or cluster can be useful.

     I. Dictator
        A. Uses fear
        B. Issues commands
     II. Cunning Manipulator
        A. Devious
        B. Turns people against each other

III. Buddy
    A. Wants to be friends
    B. Puts personal concerns above work needs
IV. Democratic Director
    A. Treats others with respect
    B. Consensus Leader

2. Avoid uninteresting phrases for your classes, such as good/average/bad, fast/medium/slow, and beautiful/ordinary/ugly.
3. Avoid overlapping classes.

    I. Dictator
    II. Cunning Manipulator
    III. Buddy
    IV. Democratic Director
    V. Ambitious (Overlapping because any of the first four could be ambitious, perhaps for different reasons.)

Transitional Words

Consider using the following transitional words to improve coherence by connecting ideas with ideas, sentences with sentences, and paragraphs with paragraphs.

FOR CLASSIFICATION:	classify, (to) group, categorize, the first class, the second class, the third class, another class, a subclass, another subclass
FOR ALL PATTERNS OF WRITING:	The HOTSHOT CAT words: *However, Otherwise, Therefore, Similarly, Hence, On the other hand, Then, Consequently, Also, Thus*

General Topics for Writing Paragraphs and Essays of Classification

1. food servers
2. dates
3. smokers
4. smiles
5. liars
6. gossips
7. sports
8. sports fans
9. churchgoers
10. laughs
11. bus drivers
12. bus or airplane passengers
13. rock music
14. hiphop music
15. texting styles
16. pick-up lines
17. chicken (or another food) eaters
18. surfers
19. beards
20. pet owners

Comparison and Contrast

One useful procedure for writing comparison-and-contrast paragraphs and essays is using the 4 *P*'s: *purpose, points, patterns,* and *presentation.*

1. **Purpose:** During the exploration of your topic, define your purpose clearly.
   - Decide whether you are writing a work that is primarily comparison, primarily contrast, or balanced.
   - Determine whether your main purpose is to inform or to persuade. For example, you might argue that one minivan is better than another.

2. **Points**
   - Indicate your points of comparison or contrast, perhaps by listing.
   - Eliminate irrelevant points.

3. **Pattern**
   - Select the subject-by-subject or the point-by-point pattern after considering your topic and planned treatment. The point-by-point pattern is usually preferred in essays. Only in long papers is there likely to be a mixture of patterns.
   - Compose an outline reflecting the pattern you select.

Subject-by-Subject Pattern

I. Subject 1
  A. Point 1
  B. Point 2

II. Subject 2
  A. Point 1
  B. Point 2

I. Nissan Quest
  A. Horsepower and gears
  B. Safety
  C. Cargo space

II. Dodge Caravan
  A. Horsepower and gears
  B. Safety
  C. Cargo space

Point-by-Point Pattern

I. Point 1
  A. Subject 1
  B. Subject 2

I. Horsepower and gears
  A. Nissan Quest
  B. Dodge Caravan

II. Point 2	II. Safety
A. Subject 1	A. Nissan Quest
B. Subject 2	B. Dodge Caravan
III. Point 3	III. Cargo space
A. Subject 1	A. Nissan Quest
B. Subject 2	B. Dodge Caravan

4. **Presentation:** Give each point more or less equal treatment. Attention to each part of the outline will usually ensure balanced development.
5. Use a carefully stated topic sentence for a paragraph and a clear thesis for an essay. Each developmental paragraph should have a topic sentence broad enough to embrace its content.
6. Consider using the following transitional words to improve coherence by connecting ideas with ideas, sentences with sentences, and paragraphs with paragraphs.

- **Comparison:** *in the same way, similarly, likewise, also, by comparison, in a like manner, as, with, as though, both, like, just as*
- **Contrast:** *but, by contrast, in contrast, despite, however, instead, nevertheless, on (to) the contrary, in spite of, still, yet, unlike, even so, rather than, otherwise*

General Topics

Select one of these topics. Make the topic specific by naming the subjects for your comparison and contrast.

1. two products, such as automobiles, bicycles, or motorcycles
2. two types of (or specific) police officers, doctors, teachers, clergy, students, or athletes
3. two roommates, neighbors, friends, or dates
4. two movies, television shows, commercials, songs, or singers
5. dating and going steady, living together and being married, or a person before and after marriage

Definition

Simple Definition

1. Keep in mind that no two words have exactly the same meaning.
2. Blend any of several forms of simple definitions into your discussion: basic dictionary definitions, synonyms, direct explanations, indirect explanations, and analytical definitions.

3. For a formal or an analytical definition, specify the term, class, and characteristic(s).

EXAMPLE <u>Capitalism</u> is <u>an economic system</u> <u>characterized by investment</u>
term   class
<u>of money, private ownership, and free enterprise.</u>
characteristics

4. Avoid "is where" and "is when" definitions, circular definitions (using forms of the word to be defined as the definition), and the use of words in the definition that are more difficult than the word being defined.

Extended Definition

1. Use listing or clustering to consider how you might use other patterns of development in defining your term. (See page 218.)
2. Decide how you will organize your writing. The organization of your extended definition is likely to be one of emphasis, but it may also be one of space or time, depending on the subject material. You may use just one pattern of development for the overall organization.
3. Consider these ways of introducing a definition: with a question, with a statement of what the word is not, with a statement of what the word originally meant, or with a discussion of why a clear definition is important. You may use a combination of these ways before you continue with your definition.
4. Consider your purpose and your audience to determine whether you will personalize a definition. Your instructor may ask you to write about a word within the context of your own experience or to write about it from a detached, clinical viewpoint.
5. Consider using the following transitional words to improve coherence by connecting ideas with ideas, sentences with sentences, and paragraphs with paragraphs.

   - *originates from, means, derives from, refers to, for example, as a term, as a concept, label, similar to, different from, in a particular context, in common usage, in historical context*

General Topics

The following topics are appropriate for extended development of definitions; most of them will also serve well for writing simple definitions.

1. role model
2. hero
3. happiness
4. cult

5. psychopath
6. successful
7. workaholic
8. street smart

9. brave
10. educated
11. cool
12. love

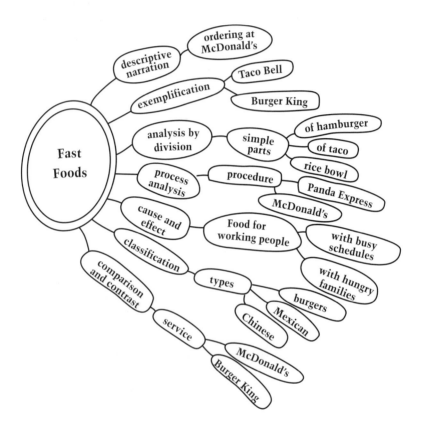

Argument

1. Ask yourself the following questions. Then consider which parts of the formal argument you should include in your paragraph or essay.

   - **Background:** What is the historical or social context for this controversial issue?
   - **Proposition** (the **thesis** of the essay): What do I want my audience to believe or to do?

- **Qualification of proposition:** Can I limit my proposition so that those who disagree cannot easily challenge me with exceptions?
- **Refutation** (taking the opposing view into account, mainly to point out its fundamental weakness): What is the view on the other side, and why is it flawed in reasoning or evidence?
- **Support:** In addition to sound reasoning, can I use appropriate facts, examples, statistics, and opinions of authorities?

2. The basic pattern of a paragraph or an essay of argument is likely to be in this form:

Proposition (the thesis of the essay)

   I. Support 1
  II. Support 2
 III. Support 3

3. Consider using the following transitional words to improve coherence by connecting ideas with ideas, sentences with sentences, and paragraphs with paragraphs.

- *it follows that, as a result, causes taken collectively, as a concession, even though, of course, in the context of, in the light of, in the final analysis, following this, further, as additional support, moreover, consequently, according to, in support of, contrary to, therefore, naturally*

General Topics

The following are broad subject areas; you will have to limit your focus for an essay of argument. You may modify the topics to fit specific situations. Consider using examples.

1. juvenile justice, treating youngsters as adults in courts
2. advertising tobacco, alcohol, and other drugs
3. casinos and state-run lotteries
4. laws for those who do graffiti in public places
5. smoking in public places: restaurants, bars, parks
6. drivers licenses for the young and the old
7. surveillance by video (on campus, in classrooms, in neighborhoods, or in shopping areas)
8. curfew for teenagers
9. laws requiring residents to maintain appearance of property
10. keeping gang members out of parks

⌒ A Variety of Writing Topics

Here are some paragraph and essay topics. For each topic that you choose, try one or more prewriting techniques, such as brainstorming, freewriting, or clustering. Then develop a strong topic sentence and a clear outline before you write, revise, and edit your paper.

1. Write about the best or the worst decision you made during the past three years.
2. Write about the breakup of a relationship. Concentrate on causes or effects.
3. Write about people's driving habits that bother you. Give some real-life examples.
4. Bring in a newspaper article of opinion (often located on the page facing the editorial page) or a letter to the editor and then agree or disagree with it in a very specific way.
5. Write your own letter to an editor of a newspaper about an issue in the news. Consider mailing your letter.
6. Write about needed changes in procedures, management, products, or services in your workplace.
7. Write about an imaginary vacation to a time and place of your choice in world history (no space-alien abduction pieces unless approved by your instructor).
8. Imagine that you have just won a million dollars in the lottery. Explain what you would do. Be specific in naming products and beneficiaries.
9. Write your job description (what you are supposed to do) in one paragraph, explaining each task as a part of your total job, and then, in an additional paragraph, explain what you really do.
10. Discuss a personal hero or role model. Emphasize the important qualities of that person.
11. Summarize a passage from a college textbook. When you summarize a passage, you rewrite it, making it shorter by about two-thirds, changing the wording without changing the information, and concentrating on main ideas. Do not add ideas, refer to yourself (by using "I"), or give your opinion. Begin by underlining the important ideas and annotating the printed material. Then construct a simple outline. Try referring only to your outline to avoid the temptation of copying material.
12. Write a detailed account of how someone helped you at a time when your self-esteem was low.

13. If you are from an immigrant family, write about what happened when your family learned about American culture by watching television soon after you arrived in this country.

14. Write about the effects television watching has had on you. How has your life changed by the amount of TV viewing you do and by your choice of programs?

15. Use the Internet to research the price, quality, style, and durability of two items that are for sale. Make copies of your data. Write a comparison-and-contrast paper explaining that one item is better than the other. Submit the computer printout along with the materials required by your instructor.

16. Write an argument either for or against the practice of using cameras in classrooms to help control bullying, cheating, bad teaching, and thefts.

17. Imagine you are leaving a job without being able to give notification. Your respected—and understanding—boss asks you to write out instructions in short essay form to help your replacement perform a task.

18. Write about a workaholic (a person who places work above all other activities and concerns) you know. Emphasize either the effects on that person and his or her family or the causes of the person's becoming fanatical about work.

19. Use one extended example of someone who is a good boss, worker, parent, coach, spouse, or neighbor.

20. Write about a crime, an accident, or a natural disaster you witnessed.

Index